Getting Started in
Speaking, Training, or Seminar Consulting

The Getting Started In Series

Getting Started in

Speaking, Training, or Seminar Consulting

Robert W. Bly

John Wiley & Sons, Inc.
New York • Chichester • Weinheim • Brisbane • Singapore • Toronto

Library of Congress Cataloging-in-Publication Data:

Bly, Robert W.
    Getting started in speaking, training, or seminar consulting / Robert W. Bly.
      p.   cm.—(The getting started in series)
    Includes index.
    ISBN 0-471-38882-3 (pbk. : alk. paper)
    1. Lectures and lecturing. 2. Public speaking. 3. Training. I. Title.
  II. Getting started in
  PN4193.L4 B56 2001
  808.5'1—dc21   00-043276

To Don Hauptman—
a good friend and great speaker

Contents

Acknowledgments

T hanks to my agent, Bonita Nelson, for finding a home for this book and to Mike Hamilton, my editor, for his patience and understanding.

Introduction

Speaking is a sometimes glamorous, high-visibility field with the potential for high income. Tom Peters, the superstar business speaker, gets $30,000 for a one-hour keynote; many top speakers earn $5,000 to $10,000 or more per day. And the market for such services is significant: According to the American Society for Training and Development, U.S. companies spend $55 billion annually on workplace training.

But you don't have to be Tom Peters, a celebrity, a motivational keynoter, or a best-selling author to make $100,000 to $400,000 a year as a professional speaker. There is a high demand today for speakers, trainers, and workshop and seminar leaders in all kinds of specialized subjects. These include everything from how to reduce stress, manage your time, supervise employees, and write a business letter to how to design a distillation column, troubleshoot a local area network, or create an e-commerce Web site.

Getting Started in Speaking, Training, or Seminar Consulting shows you, step by step, exactly what you need to do to become a polished speaker (or if you are, to become an even *better* speaker). You will learn how to create a presentation audiences want to hear, find your market, set your fees, get booked, and earn $1,000 to $5,000 a day or more as a self-employed lecturer.

It also covers the lucrative markets of corporate training and public seminars. In this book, you will discover who buys training, what topics they are looking for, how to package and sell training courses, and what to charge.

You will also discover how to create and market your own self-sponsored public seminar, write ads and mailings, and get enough paid registrations to make the event profitable. We also explore working for established seminar companies, including who the players are and how to get hired.

"To succeed requires a total commitment to your goal,"
writes Jim Donovan in his book *Handbook to a Happier Life*
(Bovan Publishing). "Keep going no matter what. If you
really believe in what you are doing, give it all you've got
and don't give up. You will succeed."

WHO CAN PROFIT FROM THIS BOOK?

Speaking, training, and leading seminars can be done either as a full-time
career or as a part-time supplemental source of income. *Getting Started in
Speaking, Training, or Seminar Consulting* can help anyone who wants to
get paid for standing in front of a group of people and telling them something they want to know, including:

✔ *Teachers.* Many teachers who burn out and look for a new career
choose speaking, because talking to adults is easier and pays better than teaching children. There are approximately 1.8 million
elementary, middle school, and high school teachers in the
United States. Teachers are such a prime market for transitioning
to training and seminars that the Learning Annex in New York
City ran a course called "Calling All Teachers: How to Get into
Training."

✔ *Consultants.* Consultants can use speaking to promote their consulting businesses as well as generate additional income (on a per
diem basis, consultants almost always make more money giving a
seminar than advising clients one-on-one).

✔ *Authors.* Like consultants, authors can use speaking to promote
their main business (writing books, articles, or newsletters) or to
generate additional income. Some authors earn more for a couple
of talks than the advance they get to write a 200-page book (like
this one!).

✔ *Corporate executives and managers.* In today's corporate environment, workers increasingly specialize in narrow areas—everything from broadband networking to cost-based accounting. This
has created a demand for seminars on these topics, which in turn
has created an unprecedented opportunity for subject matter experts to earn big money as speakers and trainers in their specialties. There is also a growing demand for seminars on engineering

Speaking is booming. In a recent poll, 58% of professional speakers surveyed said they are getting more fee-paid engagements now than in previous years.
—*The Speaking Industry Report*, Walters Speaker Services

and technical topics, and the U.S. Department of Labor's *Occupational Outlook* reports more than 1.3 million engineers working in business and industry today.

✔ *Entrepreneurs and "wanna-be" entrepreneurs.* Small business owners often promote themselves or their businesses with speaking. In the United States alone, there are more than 10 million small businesses, with 625,000 new businesses starting annually. Speaking can also turn into a nice ancillary profit center for service-based entrepreneurs. Example: Several dentists I know now make more money showing other dentists how to build their practices—through seminars, newsletters, books, and other how-to advice—than they earned themselves as full-time dentists.

✔ *Training professionals.* Training managers and corporate trainers see how much money they are paying freelance trainers, and many decide to make the transition. In the United States, corporations employ more than 20,000 full-time training managers and thousands of others who do training part-time as part of their overall job descriptions.

✔ *Professional speakers and aspiring speakers.* The National Speakers Association, a group for professional and aspiring speakers, has 4,000 members. The total number of wanna-be speakers may be as high as 10 times this number, based on my observation of how many nonmembers attend local NSA functions in the metropolitan New York area near my office.

Whether you see speaking as a means of self-promotion, an occasional way to earn a nice fat fee, a vehicle for educating others, or something you want to pursue on a regular basis, *Getting Started in Speaking, Training, or Seminar Consulting* can help make your dream a reality.

You can get paid to stand up in front of a group and talk. It's enjoyable, and one of the highest-paying professions when fees are calculated on a per-hour basis.

You can help people change their lives for the better—and get them to give you a standing ovation at the same time.

You'll establish a reputation as an authority in your field. Others will seek you out for your counsel. The media will ask you to write for them, will write about you, and have you as a guest on TV and radio shows.

Corporations and associations will pay you to travel all over the world and stay in the top hotels in the most beautiful cities and resort destinations. What could be more fun, exciting, or rewarding?

Overview of the Speaking, Training, and Seminar Business

There are a lot of people who want to be speakers today—but perhaps some of them should not. This book will help you determine if speaking is for you and, if it is, how you can get good, get hired, and get paid.

Many would-be speakers have a burning desire to stand before and address a crowd. Having the desire to speak is great—and it puts you in the minority of Americans, since poll after poll shows that most Americans dislike, even fear, public speaking. So if you desire rather than fear public speaking, that's a good start.

Other would-be speakers are more interested in the rewards of speaking. They imagine themselves before a cheering group, collecting a big standing ovation—and a big fat check after they are done. That's nice, too. But if you're speaking to get applause, you're speaking for the wrong reason.

The key reason to be a speaker, in my opinion, should be to share your understanding of a subject in which you have knowledge, expertise, and experience, and for which you have love and passion. Your mission should be to motivate people—that is, to get others as excited about your topic as you are.

It should also be to shorten their learning curve: By sharing what you know, you can help your audience learn, in minutes or hours, tips

5

and insights that took you years of trial and error to master. This is the sole reason why people attend seminars and speeches: to take shortcuts in the learning process by tapping into the knowledge of those more experienced than themselves.

My problem with the seminar and speaking business as I see it practiced today, both at the novice and at the professional level, is that the focus is on being a speaker rather than being a subject matter expert. The best speakers—by that, I mean those who impart the most value to their audiences—are experts who share their knowledge in many ways, speaking being just one of them.

There are too many people who decide to be a professional speaker, then go out looking for a topic on which to speak.

For example, at a recent meeting of the National Speakers Association (NSA), I sat next to a man who came because he wanted to become a speaker. "What topic interests you?" I asked. "Leadership," he replied. "What do you do now?" I asked. He replied, "I am a janitor at the high school." Did he lead a service organization, church, community group, or scout troop? No. Then why did he choose leadership as his specialty? "Because the magazines I read say leadership is a hot topic now," he replied. Why did he feel competent on the subject? Because, he informed me, he had just read two books about it.

Now, there's nothing wrong with being a high school janitor. But the men and women who attend his speeches will be dedicated entrepreneurs running growing businesses, or high-level executives in big corporations. Many will be earning six-figure salaries; some will be millionaires. How can this man stand before a corporate chief executive officer or dot-com billionaire and tell them how to be leaders, when he takes his orders from the secretary of the assistant vice principal? It's a lie, it's dishonest, it's not credible, and it's the heart of what's wrong with the speaking industry today.

Learn something first, and be better at your subject than anyone else. Then you can offer audiences a unique value other speakers in your field cannot match.

This focus on subject rather than speaking is a contrarian viewpoint that many professional and would-be speakers might disagree with, or even be offended by. So be it. You will find this is a contrarian book throughout. While I count many professional speakers as friends and colleagues, a lot of what goes on in the field today is harmful instead of beneficial to the customers—that is, the listening audience. I strive to correct that, and to make you the kind of speaker who contributes to the correction of that deficiency rather than promulgates it, whenever I can. Why?

Your career—and the status of the speaking profession—will ultimately improve as a result.

WHAT DO WE MEAN BY A SEMINAR VERSUS A TRAINING PROGRAM OR WORKSHOP?

There are a number of subcategories within the speaking profession.

Professional speakers typically focus on shorter presentations (anywhere from 30 minutes to two hours, with an hour being common) to larger audiences. Often speakers focus on motivation and topics of broad interest: sales, leadership, e-business.

Seminar leaders specialize in longer formats—typically full-day programs—in front of smaller audiences, and their programs are on more focused and specialized topics: anything from business writing and grammar to customer service skills and Visual Basic. They usually teach either a skill (how to use Word) or a process (how to start your own business).

Trainers focus on doing private seminars in soft skills (etiquette, ethics, coping with difficult people), hard skills (printed circuit board design, cost-based accounting, inventory management), or business and regulatory issues (preparing for ISO certification, passing an OSHA—Occupational Safety and Health Administration—inspection) for corporate clients. They typically train groups of 15 to 30 employees at a time in half-day, full-day, or two-day seminars on the client's premises or at a nearby hotel the client has arranged. Ask them what they do and they will usually answer, "I am in training," and not "I'm a professional speaker."

For convenience, in the box I give definitions of the various formats (speech, seminar, workshop, training, etc.) and types of speakers.

These categories are not rigid. Many speakers, trainers, and seminar leaders do a mix of different types of presentations to different audiences. For simplicity, from this point on I will generally refer to anyone who speaks, teaches, or trains as a "speaker."

WHO IS DOING IT?

Writer May Sarton once said, "Everyone wants to have written a book, but few people actually want to sit down and write one." In the same way, many people want to give speeches before a group, but few people want to

Speech. A lecture, usually 20 to 90 minutes, given before a group of from 10 to 1,000 or more. Speeches are somewhat formal. The speaker reads a prepared lecture or follows an outline of points to cover. Audience participation is minimal and usually confined to a brief question-and-answer session after the talk. Audiovisual aids are usually not used. *Example:* The U.S. president's State of the Union address.

Keynote. A keynote is a speech that is the main speech at a meeting or for that day of the meeting. Keynote speakers command big fees, and usually speak to the entire group of meeting attendees at or after breakfast, lunch, or dinner. A keynote speech is typically 30 to 90 minutes and usually focuses on a broad topic of interest to all attendees. *Example:* At an advertising association meeting, science fiction writer Ray Bradbury gave a keynote on creativity.

Breakout session. One of the side sessions during a meeting, as opposed to the keynote session. Often meetings will be broken into "tracks"—sequences of breakout sessions each following a different theme or topic. Most breakout sessions are from 45 to 90 minutes. Two or three breakouts are typically held simultaneously. Attendees may go to the ones that interest them most. Therefore, total attendance at breakouts is less than at keynotes, and breakout speakers often command a lesser fee than a keynoter. *Example:* At the annual meeting of a printing industry association, a sales trainer giving a breakout on how to use cold calls to get new accounts.

Presentation. Similar to a speech, but usually longer and less structured. Multimedia audiovisual aids are often used, and there is more audience participation. A presentation usually covers one topic, often with the goal of bringing members of a team up to speed on a project or issue, and getting resolution so as to move forward. *Example:* An engineer explaining the technology of a new product to the marketing department so that they may develop a plan to market the technology.

Seminar. A presentation on a topic covering some facet of knowledge or skill (e.g., banking regulations, telemarketing, quality control, digital imaging). The program can be public or private (see "training"). The presentation is usually organized into modules. The speaker's goal is to impart knowledge of the topic, and he or she typically uses a combination of lecture, visual aids, interaction with participants, and exercises to get the job done.

Workshop. Similar to a seminar but with a greater degree of attendee participation, interaction, and hands-on exercises. A seminar may convey the fundamentals of Web site design, but at a workshop on the subject, trainees may actually design Web pages during the class, and even walk away with their finished Web site on disk as part of the program.

Training. Training refers to seminars or workshops conducted for a private client, usually a corporation, specifically for a group of its employees. Most corporate training seminars are one or two days.

Public seminar. A seminar where registration is open to the general public. Most are one day; some are two or three days or even longer.

Professional speaker. A person who gets paid a fee (beyond the nominal honorarium some amateur speakers receive) for giving speeches, presentations, workshops, seminars, and training courses.

Amateur speaker. A speaker who speaks for pure enjoyment or to promote his or her company (or self), rather than for a speaking fee.

Full-time speaker. A professional speaker who speaks frequently enough to earn a sufficient amount of money to support himself or herself solely or primarily from speaking and related activities (e.g., sales of training materials and products).

Part-time speaker. An amateur or professional speaker who speaks occasionally, and for whom speaking is not the primary career.

do the preparation required to get to the point where they deserve to be invited to give that talk.

Many speakers are driven by a desire to talk, but for the talk to be worth someone else's listening, you have to have something worthwhile to say.

The people who make the best speakers have valuable experience in a particular field or task, augmented by further study into that specialty and topped off with a desire to share it, a knack for teaching, and the ability to say things in a clear, entertaining way.

Take an inventory of your life and career. First, do you have experience that others can learn from? Actually, most of us do. Did you retire successfully at age 40? Many people will pay to hear how you did it—both how you made enough money to accomplish that early retirement, as well as how you managed to cope with going from hard worker to man or woman of leisure.

Any significant life experience that others have also had, want to know about, or can learn something useful from can serve as the starting point for putting together a talk others will pay you to give. These can include personal experiences as well as business and career knowledge gained on the job. They can be dramatic (you survived nearly freezing to death climbing Mount Everest) or everyday (you gave up a high-pressure job on Wall Street to raise your triplets on a farm in the country).

Notice I didn't say anything about having a burning desire to speak, because that alone doesn't qualify you. Don't start with you as speaker. Start with you and your information. What's your topic? Or more effectively, start with your experiences: What topic of interest to a business audience (and the majority of speaking is done for and paid for by businesses, specifically corporations) or the general public does your experience qualify you to speak about?

There is intense competition in professional speaking today, as there is in nearly every other field. Speaking in particular is extra competitive because so many people want to do it. So if you decide you are simply interested in "customer service" as a topic—because either it's the flavor of the week or it seems easy to do—you have a problem: What makes you different or better than the zillion other consultants out there who are all offering customer service programs to the same corporate audience?

Experience is the strongest differentiator you can have, one that adds credibility to listeners during your talk as well as to potential clients when you pitch your speaking services. *Example:* I have a cousin who asked me about whether he should go into speaking, talking about customer service. He was at the time a concierge at a major hotel. Who works harder than a concierge to meet customer needs? I suggested to him that if he marketed a customer service program to the hospitality and travel industries, he could write his own ticket.

That's the way you should launch your speaking career: from experience and aimed at a specific market. The more experience you have in the topic, the more credible you are versus other speakers. Even better, the more experience you have in the client's industry (or something close to it), the more inclined the client will be to hire you over speakers who do not specialize in an industry.

Earlier I talked about the school janitor who wanted to speak on leadership to corporate CEOs, and the reasons I believe he is not qualified and will not succeed. He should ask, "What *do* I know?" Do the teenagers at his high school confide in him, and have him help them with their problems? Did he help a teen drug dealer get on the straight path and become a community leader, or a suicidal computer nerd become a dot-com billionaire? Perhaps his topic should be "Helping Teens Succeed in School and in Life," and he should focus on the education market, talking to parents through seminars sponsored by school systems.

If you have experience, a topic, and an audience, then ask yourself, "Am I eager to speak?" Probably you are already, or you would not be reading this book. Most speakers enjoy both the idea of speaking as well as the act itself. They may get butterflies before they go onstage, but on the platform they have fun.

There are many easier ways to make a living than speaking. If you have not already given a speech, do some freebies for local business associations, at work, or for community groups. If you don't enjoy it, why would you want to do this for a living? If you have the jitters or are awkward, that's okay: You'll get better as you do more. But if the whole thing causes you to be miserable or doesn't turn you on, maybe it's not for you.

Most speakers are also "closet scholars": They enjoy reading, researching, and learning, usually in many areas but certainly in their chosen speaking specialty. If you are bored and burned-out in your field, and are thinking of coasting by delivering the same old information you learned years ago, you may want to reconsider speaking as a career choice. Good speakers are turned on by learning, and constantly research and read about their topic to learn more. If you are no longer a student of your topic, you should not be taking on students of your own. As the old saying goes, "School is never out for the pro."

Other qualifications? You don't have to be an extrovert or people person—many speakers I know of, including me, are very private people—

Write down the three biggest problems that people in the audiences to whom you'd like to speak have. Then write down the experiences you have, the major projects you've handled, the subjects you have studied, and the skills you have. When you can match an area of your own experience or knowledge with the needs of a target audience, you are on your way to defining a speaking niche for yourself.

but you should care about people, have a desire to help them, and be comfortable with them. I am a loner by nature, but I get a real kick out of seeing people react to what I tell them, and even more of a kick when they contact me later to tell me they got results using my methods. The fact that I don't want to go to a barbecue with them doesn't interfere with my value to them as a speaker or my relationship with them as a client.

ADVANTAGES

I said in the introduction to this book that speaking can be a glamorous profession, and to some degree that's true. Here are the five major benefits of speaking, either as a full-time profession or as a spare-time second source of income:

1. *It pays well.* Speakers earn thousands of dollars per speech. Top earners who specialize in short programs can make $3,000 an hour or more based on their actual speaking time. Often speakers earn many more times the money that the managers and executives in their audiences— who often work much harder and are not as appreciated—earn. According to an article in the *Record* (March 3, 2000), former president George Bush and wife Barbara earned a combined $6 million in speaking fees in 1999. Computer author Esther Dyson earned $1.2 million, and retired general Colin Powell made $3 million.

2. *You are treated with respect.* Compared with consultants, vendors, repair services, and other suppliers clients hire, speakers get pretty good treatment; many people actually fawn over them. Because of the high fees they command and the fact they are not part of the corporate structure, many people hang on their every word. Also, since they give advice but do not implement it, they get all the glory whether their ideas work or not, and almost none of the blame if they don't.

3. *You travel the world at someone else's expense.* Speakers are flown and put up, all expenses paid, in some exotic locations, often at world-class hotels. As I write this, I sit in Newark Airport, awaiting a flight—ticket paid for by a corporate client—to give seminars in Bonn and Warsaw, two places I might not otherwise have visited.

4. *You gain a reputation as an expert in your field.* Speaking is prestigious and builds your reputation as an expert in a particular area. This in turn brings more speaking opportunities at even higher fees, as well as other benefits ranging from media appearances to being invited to teach at a university, contribute to major magazines, or even write books—all of which helps your star rise even higher.

5. *You get paid to study.* Most of the people in your audience are too busy handling day-to-day tasks to delve into the theory and news of their field of specialty in anything more than the most casual inquiry. As the speaker and authority in the field, you get high fees from clients, while you have the unbelievable luxury of not doing the fine details day to day, but instead focusing on the big picture—through reading, research, surveys, observation, thinking, and writing. Film critic Roger Ebert said that his father, an electrician at a university, never taught him electrical work because he believed the professors had it so much easier: "They sit back with their feet on the desk, read books, and smoke pipes." As a speaker, you get to be the professor, not the electrician.

DISADVANTAGES

Of course, the life of a professional speaker is not all champagne and caviar, and sometimes the same five items that are advantages can also be disadvantages:

1. *Money.* Yes, you get paid. When you speak. But even many experienced speakers don't actually do much speaking. Most of their time is spent marketing, prospecting, following up, closing, traveling, researching, and creating—most of which they don't get paid for. Most consultants spend 50 to 60 percent of their time on work directly billable to clients, but I suspect this figure may be lower for most speakers.

2. *Respect.* While many people respect speakers as gurus, others ridicule or disrespect them for the same qualities. Some people resent or even have contempt for speakers, seeing them as overpaid blowhards who talk big but never actually do anything. The more of a practitioner you are versus just a theoretician, the more you will be exempt from the particular criticism that "those who can, do; those who can't, teach."

Speaking is not always a bed of roses. Like anything else, it has both advantages and disadvantages. Be glad for the disadvantages; if it were easy, everyone would do it. As I read recently on a poster, "You can either complain that rosebushes have thorns—or rejoice that thorn bushes have roses."

3. *Travel.* Anyone who has done any substantial business travel knows it is at least as much of a curse as it is a blessing. Even the most travel-seeking novice speakers soon tire of airplane food, canceled flights, cramped cabins, airport delays, and driving to unfamiliar cities at 2 A.M. in a rented car. And while you may visit some exotic places, often your busy schedule will ensure that the only sites you see are the convention hotel and the highway between it and the airport.

4. *Reputation.* You can build a stellar reputation, but you never know when the next business trend will render your presentation and content old hat. Look at Tom Peters. "Excellence" made his reputation, but then he had to invent something new to sell: "liberation management." I think he's on his third or fourth trend now. For the experienced practitioner with a solid knowledge base, having to continually keep up with trends or add a new twist to the speech can get wearisome.

5. *Study.* The best part of being a speaker is you always get to study your topic, all the time. The worst part of being a speaker is you always have to study your topic, all the time. It's fun, but it's hard work that often goes unappreciated.

HOW MUCH MONEY CAN YOU MAKE?

Oscar Wilde said, "Expense is one thing you can't get for nothing." A part-time speaker who does 20 to 30 fee-paid presentations a year and charges $4,000 per seminar will earn an extra $80,000 to $120,000 in speaking fees. A full-time speaker who does double this volume and sells training materials—workbooks, software, and audio- or video-tape albums—can make $200,000 to $500,000 a year or more. The top non-celebrity trainers and speakers might make over $500,000 a year. For the novice who wants to pursue speaking as a full-time profession, it's reasonable to expect to gross $100,000 to $200,000 annually within the first few years.

HOW LONG WILL IT TAKE TO TURN A PROFIT?

Professional speaking requires a relatively modest investment at the beginning; you can get started with just business cards, letterhead, and a promotional circular on your talks. As you get more experience, you can invest some of your profits back into the business, especially in more professional marketing materials.

While the start-up expenses are small, the start-up period tends to last anywhere from six months to a year or longer. To get good enough to speak professionally, you have to start speaking when you are not so good, and usually the only way to do this is to speak for free (see Chapter 4). But it takes time and effort even to book these free speaking engagements, and the lead time is often two or three months.

So it takes a while to get good, get started, and get established to the point where people are willing to pay you. This is why I advise beginners to get into speaking part-time and keep their day jobs. It may be a year or two until your speaking income exceeds your regular paycheck and you can seriously consider quitting your day job to pursue a full-time speaking career.

The time investment to become a speaker is greatest in the first year. Reason: You must spend an enormous amount of time creating your presentations, including research, content, and handouts. The investment in creating this material is amortized over the number of times you sell and give this presentation to clients, which for most speakers is a considerable return on investment.

HOW MUCH MONEY WILL IT COST TO START?

If you don't have a lick of computer equipment or any desk space in your home you can use as an office, your start-up costs will be around $5,000 to $7,000. If you already own a desk, file cabinet, personal computer (PC), fax, and copier, your investment can be as little as a few hundred dollars for letterhead, business cards, and envelopes. Other start-up costs include having a good photo taken of you, making up a sales sheet or promotional flyer on your speech, and having a demo tape. You can start with audio, but as you get good and start moving up to higher-paying venues, you'll want to spend a few hundred dollars to a thousand dollars on a video demo.

CAN I DO THIS FROM MY HOME?

Most professional speakers have their offices at home. Since you always visit the client to deliver your service (the speech), there's no need to have clients visit you; and therefore, having professional-looking offices isn't necessary. That's a big advantage over other professional service businesses, such as dentists and therapists, where the client comes to your office.

CAN I DO IT IN MY SPARE TIME?

Speaking can be pursued as a full-time job or spare-time second source of income.

Most books focus on full-time speaking, but I agree with speakers like Earl Nightingale and Mike Aun that every speaker should have another job. Even speakers like John Naisbitt and Tom Peters aren't really full-time speakers; they are full-time researchers and writers who find speaking a very lucrative avenue for sharing what they learn with a wider audience.

I once went to a convention where one of the speakers was an old-time speaker, well known but not in touch with what the speaking business is like today. He gave the same motivational, canned talk he must have given three thousand times before, and it was pitiful to watch. As the disinterested audience dispersed after cursory clapping at the end, the speaker made a half-hearted pitch, asking us to pick up brochures so we could buy his tapes. The brochures remained scattered on a table, and no one stayed to talk with the speaker or ask questions.

To be relevant, you have to be involved—in your skill area, craft,

Do you want to pursue speaking but feel you don't have enough time given your full-time job and other responsibilities? From this moment on, vow not to watch television. You have just put the extra time you need back into your life.

trade, industry, or technical discipline—whether it's as a businessperson, entrepreneur, consultant, or author. Speaker Mike Aun, for example, runs a successful insurance business; Dan Poynter, who speaks on publishing, owns a publishing company.

If your goal is to speak so much that you never do anything else, you may want to rethink your goal; otherwise, you risk lapsing into irrelevance.

CAN I DO THIS IF I AM NOT A RISK TAKER OR HAVE A LIMITED BUDGET?

Unlike starting a restaurant, creating a product, or launching an e-business, becoming a professional speaker does not involve large risks. You invest very little money, and if it doesn't work out, no one will ever know. If your efforts yield modest results and only a few engagements, you can do those jobs in your spare time and earn some nice extra income. On the other hand, if you start a restaurant and it fails, everyone knows about it.

Most speakers I know are not tremendous risk takers. A much more important quality than risk taking for would-be speakers is persistence. Those who keep at it eventually reach some level of results. Those who give up early never get the speaking opportunities they seek.

Chapter

Picking a Topic

A professional speaker is one who is paid for his or her time. Therefore, amateur speakers—those who are not paid—have much more leeway in choice of topic than do professionals.

The amateur can speak on any topic—ranging from aromatherapy to zoology and anything in between—that might interest a group of people or a sponsor. Typical sponsors can include town libraries, chambers of commerce, service clubs (Elks and Rotary), Toastmasters, local museums, cultural societies, book clubs, even Boy Scout troops.

The topic doesn't have to be important or valuable enough for someone actually to pay for—since the amateur speaker isn't paid. It merely has to be interesting enough for people to want to spend an hour listening to it (actually no small feat given people's busy schedules and the glut of other subjects and media competing for each listener's attention).

The professional speaker, if he or she is to make a good living, must speak on topics that businesspeople are interested in and that businesses—or associations whose members are businesses or professionals—are willing to pay for. Usually this means speaking on business, technical, and professional topics, such as customer service, hiring, proposal writing, sales, or meeting OSHA regulations. These topics are so interesting and vital that the companies hiring the speakers will pay them fees that often work out to hundreds or even thousands of dollars per hour for the actual presentation—far more than the attendees in the audience earn.

Increasingly at business and association meetings, especially large meetings with multiple presentations, the sponsor will hire one or two speakers to do nonbusiness topics for the business audiences. Typically these are motivational speakers and humorists. Sometimes a fitness guru is hired to talk about exercise or lead a workout session. Today I got a mailing for a conference of technologists; the luncheon speaker was humor writer Dave Barry.

At a conference for dentists on how to build a lucrative practice, where I was one of many speakers on marketing, a fitness coach gave a motivational talk centered around keeping fit to have more energy. He made a point of telling the audience he had been tested and found to have only 8 percent body fat, which apparently is considered low.

I followed him, and I am slightly chunky. I told the audience, "I have eight percent fat . . . just in my little finger!"—and got a good laugh. You can often connect with the audience by playing off something a previous speaker said or did. Just do it in a complementary manner; never insult, put down, or argue with points made by any other speaker the group has hired.

WHAT MAKES A GOOD TOPIC?

When would-be speakers start investigating the field, many quickly find a gap between what they want to talk about and what audiences want to hear. You naturally want to talk about what interests you. But those who hire speakers want presentations on topics of interest to their audiences. If your interests and the audiences' are not the same, they will not hire you anyway simply because you are eloquent and articulate; they want to know what they want to know, not what you want to tell them.

For the professional speaker targeting a business audience, topics are generally either broad or niche. Broad topics are of universal appeal or near-universal appeal to business audiences. Management and sales are the two perennial favorites. Offshoots include leadership, teamwork, motivation, customer service, and marketing.

Niche topics are those that fill a specialized need by targeting a particular subject to a particular audience: marketing for chiropractors, presentation skills for women, technical writing for engineers, stress management for tax accountants, business management for dentists. In fact, speaking to dentists is such a large niche, I once got a mailing from a woman who said she was a speaking coach and speaker's bureau specializing exclusively in dental speaking!

A speaker's bureau is an agency that matches speakers with clients needing presentations. The bureau gets a 25 to 30 percent commission for making the match, which comes out of the speaker's fee.

There is a brisk demand for broad and niche topics and speakers who can deliver them. The broad topics have a larger audience, of course—since they are, by nature, universal—but also more competition. Some speakers prefer broad topics because they allow the speaker to concentrate on the pure discipline (e.g., listening skills) without dealing with the idiosyncrasies of a particular profession or field (e.g., listening skills for arbitrators).

The niche topics have a narrower audience but less competition. There may be a zillion sales speakers, but only a few specialize in the printing industry. So by targeting a niche you reduce the competition and have greater appeal to your target audience. Speakers who prefer niche topics like the fact that they know the audience's needs and special problems thoroughly, and therefore can deliver practical, targeted advice and techniques, not just general methods or theories.

Roxanne Emmerich is a talented professional speaker whose presentation on "business breakthroughs" is a combination of sales, marketing, and customer service. Having been a banking executive, she has developed a niche program, "banking breakthroughs," which she targets to banks and bank associations. She also has a generic version that covers breakthroughs in all industries other than banking. But because of her reputation, experience, and credibility in the banking industry, you can see the advantage she has when selling the banking program to banking prospects. Think about it. If you were the training manager at a bank, who would you hire? Roxanne Emmerich, who has dozens of banks on her client list and is herself the owner of a bank holding company? Or Joe Blow, who has a generic customer service program and, when asked if he has banking experience, mumbles something about no, but the principles are really the same for every industry?

Having a niche topic in one's own industry, then creating a generic program for other industries, is a strategy that works well for speakers who have spent their previous careers within one industry. Their career experience makes them attractive to clients within the industry, giving them an edge over speakers who do not have a niche within the industry.

Needed and Wanted

A good topic is both wanted and needed by the potential audience and seminar sponsor. *Needed* means it's important: Not having the skill or knowledge creates problems that cost the business time or money.

Sometimes this need is obvious. When articles and books on a particular subject start proliferating, you know there is a need for information on the topic. Speaker bureaus will get a sharp increase in the number of requests for talks on that topic. When unemployment is low and everyone has a job, for instance, employers have a more difficult time hiring people, and want speakers to talk about hiring and employee retention.

Other times, the need is not so obvious, and you have to be clever about fitting the program you offer to the needs of an audience. Example: I give seminars in technical writing, normally to engineers. But I realized that pharmaceutical companies had a need to write clearly when submitting drugs for Food and Drug Administration approval. A test promotion I did offering a seminar on "Technical Writing for FDA Submissions" pulled a 3 percent response and generated immediate business.

If your potential customer doesn't see the topic as needed and important, it will be difficult to sell the prospect on hiring you. The higher the topic (or, more accurately, the problem the topic addresses) is on the buyer's list of priorities, the easier it will be for you to get hired.

It's good if people need your topic, but even better if they want it, too. *Wanted* means it's desired: The companies want to sponsor seminars on the topic, and even better, the audience wants to attend them and, learn the knowledge.

When I am teaching writing skills to engineers, most of the engineers in the class don't want to be there. They think writing is unimportant, and they are only there because their supervisor enrolled them in the course.

On the other hand, when I teach public seminars on how to get a book published, all the people in the audience have paid out of their own pockets. They want to write a book and get it published, are interested in the topic, and eager to spend time with a published author who has done what they want to do. They want to be there.

Soft Skills versus Hard Skills

Another distinction in topics is soft skills versus hard skills.

Soft skills are disciplines that are nontechnical in nature and do not require a specialized background to practice. Examples include listening, leadership, supervision, time management, negotiating, stress management, and business writing.

Hard skills are disciplines that are technical in nature and require specialized background or training to practice. Examples include local area network (LAN) administration, engine repair, computer troubleshooting, software development, bookkeeping, and tax preparation.

There is a brisk demand for both hard and soft skills, but more competition in soft skills. After all, anyone theoretically can teach time management, but how many of us are qualified to give a seminar on distillation column design? Therefore, presenters of hard skill subjects often can charge more than soft skill instructors, because they offer a program the client cannot easily get elsewhere.

HOW DO YOU FIND THE RIGHT TOPIC FOR YOU?

Aristotle said, "Where the needs of the world and your talents cross, there lies your vocation." In the same way, where the needs of an audience and your interest and expertise cross, your speaking topic may be found.

On the one hand, you have subjects that interest you. You can be interested in any topic you want. But that doesn't guarantee you an audience and platform on which you can lecture about the topic.

Speaking is, for many people, only satisfying if they can do it for an audience. Thousands of people who play the piano do so for their own enjoyment only, and feel no need to perform on a stage or a recording. They enjoy the music they make, as well as the act of making it, without a public forum. But speakers crave an audience; we don't like talking unless someone is listening.

The trick is to take an inventory of your possible topics, then see which of these may hold some appeal for a paying audience.

List your subjects. When taking inventory of your knowledge, ask yourself these questions:

- ✔ What skills do I have?
- ✔ What industries have I worked in?
- ✔ What positions and jobs have I had?
- ✔ What degrees do I hold?
- ✔ What subjects have I studied?

✔ What specialized training have I had?

✔ What are my hobbies?

When you go through this process, you may find that you know many more things than you thought you did. For instance, one speaker's list looked like this:

✔ Have a bachelor of science degree in mechanical engineering.

✔ Am an experienced technical manager.

✔ Speak a foreign language.

✔ Know HTML (Hypertext Markup Language) and can design Web pages.

✔ Have worked in the defense and chemical processing industries.

✔ Have done photography.

✔ Possess good leadership qualities.

✔ Possess good project management skills.

✔ Can operate a forklift.

✔ Am the parent of three teenage boys.

✔ Am a stock market investor.

You can immediately see topics begin to suggest themselves, just by combining items on the list. If this individual is very successful in stock market investing, but as an engineer takes a conservative approach that would appeal to engineers, maybe he or she can speak on personal finance to engineers, both for associations and companies that employ engineers.

Now make a list of the topics you might want to speak about. The more these topics are based on the education, training, and experience you listed earlier, the better your chances for success: Clients increasingly want speakers who have credentials and real-world experience in their topics. Speakers who have merely learned about the topic through self-study at the library and on the Internet are at a disadvantage. Be the former, not the latter.

The next step is to analyze whether there is an audience for one or more of the topics on your list. For instance, suppose you want to speak on "How to Quit Your Corporate Job and Start Your Own Business." Lots of people are interested, but does a corporate employer want to pay you to encourage valuable employees to leave their jobs? Probably not, so

A young man who desired to become a speaker complained to me that he couldn't find a topic because he didn't possess any special expertise. He said the only job he had held was as a concierge in hotels. He now speaks on customer service in the hospitality (hotel and travel) industries, a huge niche market.

you have to find another venue for such a program: One might be a public seminar.

Similarly, if you offered to teach engineers how to invest better, the employer might not feel it's a good investment of its own money to teach employees to play the stock market; perhaps the firm would prefer that employees invest only in the company's own sponsored retirement plan.

On the other hand, if you could teach engineers leadership skills, firms that promote engineers to management positions would probably find that desirable and valuable. So "Leadership Skills for Technical Professionals" is a topic for which you might find a market.

WHAT ARE THE HOT-SELLING TOPICS RIGHT NOW?

I have mixed feelings about answering this question. Here's why: Speakers who happen to speak on a subject that is or becomes a hot topic can do very, very well financially.

However, for you to pursue a topic as your own simply because it is a hot topic is probably not a good idea.

The best topics to speak on are subjects about which you have knowledge, experience, and, most importantly, passion.

If meditation suddenly becomes a hot topic and you've been meditating for decades, by all means put together a program on it, and cash in on the trend. You may do very well with it.

On the other hand, if you've never meditated and have in fact scorned meditation as New Age nonsense, don't suddenly study it and offer a program simply because it's now trendy. Your insincerity and lack of real enthusiasm will show through. You'll have difficulty getting speaking gigs, and when you do, you probably will deliver a lackluster presentation—again, your disdain and inexperience will be evident.

Speaking is to some degree a fad-driven business. Being able to anticipate a fad or trend and offer the topic before it becomes trendy can put a lot of money in your pocket. But it's extremely difficult to pull off, and few do it.

Most of us get excited about a trend and decide to cash in on it when it's already popular. By the time we develop a program to take advantage of it, the trend is fading, demand is slow, and the money has already been made by innovators who got in early.

There have been many training trends over the years. When I first worked in corporations in the late 1970s, some of the fads included productivity improvement and something called quality circles. More recent trends have included total quality management, reengineering, and ISO 9000. As this book is being written, anything to do with the Internet, the World Wide Web, e-commerce, and e-business are hot, as is something called customer relationship management (CRM). Tomorrow . . . who knows?

WHICH TOPICS ARE "EVERGREEN" (POPULAR ALL THE TIME)?

There are three topics that, in some form or another, are always in demand:

1. *Management.* Companies always want to help their employees become better managers. Leadership, teamwork, supervisory skills, customer service, conflict resolution, negotiation, interpersonal skills, and communications skills are always in demand.

2. *Selling.* There is a huge market for sales training, and also lots of trainers competing for these contracts. The appeal is tangible return on training investment: If you can help a $100 million company increase sales only 1 percent, your $5,000 seminar can help the client generate revenue of $1 million—paying back your fee 200 times over!

3. *Compliance.* Laws and regulations change frequently and are confusing; regulatory agencies are bureaucratic and difficult to deal with. Trainers who teach companies and employees how to comply with federal, state, local, and industry regulations have a continuous market. And the payback from training is tangible: avoidance of fines and other penalties imposed when regulations are violated.

CAN YOU GIVE A TALK ON ANY TOPIC YOU CHOOSE?

Speakers require no license, permit, or other certification to offer and render speaking services. (There may be exceptions in certain specialized fields, but I am not aware of them.) So the answer is, if you can convince someone to hire you to give the speech, you can talk on that topic.

Speakers differ on whether anyone can truly speak on any subject. One school says, "Anyone can study up on a topic, learn it, and teach it to others." These speakers feel the key qualification is the ability to entertain and inform on the platform; the subject matter is secondary and can be learned. At least one large public seminar company I know holds to this belief. The company hires seminar presenters who are not subject matter experts, supplying them with existing seminars they are expected to learn.

The opposite school, which I feel more aligned with, believes the audience has a right, and should demand, that speakers be experts in their subjects. Yes, you can be given a canned seminar, learn it, and perhaps deliver it reasonably well. But without the in-depth knowledge and experience in the subject, you can't speak authoritatively. Nor can you reply to questions with real confidence that your answer is correct, or give meaningful help to attendees with specific problems and concerns.

Many authors do speaking to promote their books or to make additional income from their topics, and the public perceives book authors to be experts. But actually, I believe you need to be more of an expert to speak on a subject than to write a book on it! The book author can always act as a journalist and interview experts, then write up the results as a section of a chapter devoted to that subtopic. But speakers don't have teams of experts in the room with them when they talk; they have

To get into a particular industry, join its major trade association. If you do not qualify as a regular member, often you can join as a "vendor" at a reduced rate. When you send a prospecting letter to potential clients in the association, address it "Dear Fellow XYZ Association Member." They will pay more attention because they see you as a colleague.

to have enough knowledge to answer questions on the subtopic without assistance.

What kinds of credentials are required to teach a particular subject? Unlike a public schoolteacher, you don't need an education degree or other formal credentials to lead a seminar. However, professional recognition and accreditations are certainly a plus when marketing your speaking services to potential clients. So if you are a professional engineer or a Certified Novell Administrator, highlight this in your bios and promotional materials. Not having the degree or certificate, though, will not be a barrier to success.

EVALUATING YOUR TOPIC'S MARKET POTENTIAL

One way to test-market a topic is to create a small test mailing and send it out to potential clients. Direct mail experts say you need to mail 5,000 pieces to get a statistically valid test, but you can get a good feel for your program's appeal by mailing as few as 100 or 200 letters. When I test-marketed "Technical Writing for FDA Submissions," I mailed 200 letters, got back six reply cards (a 3 percent response), and sold two one-day seminars for a total of $6,000 in fees. Based on these results and even the interest shown by the prospects who responded but didn't buy immediately (some did not have the budget), I knew I had a winner.

You could also do a market test using telemarketing, and, you can tell people about your new program at meetings, conferences, and networking events. Another way to test the waters is to post a seminar description on your Web site, perhaps with a banner on your home page highlighting the new offering. If people click, read, and request more information, or e-mail you with questions, you can judge whether the idea has some life to it.

An advantage we have in the speaking business is that we can "dry-test" new topics, meaning to put out feelers through a test marketing cam-

If you are doing several test mailings, add a key code in the return reply card to indicate which mailing generated each reply. For example, "Dept. STC7" could mean the July mailing to members of the Society for Technical Communication (STC).

> Our lives are filled with choices. We worry: What if I choose the wrong mate and our marriage ends in divorce? What if I eat too much over the holidays and gain weight? What if I choose the wrong career and I'm bored the rest of my life? We don't have to worry. God allows course corrections!
> —Terry Whalin, *Love Psalms* (Honor Books)

paign before the program has actually been developed. Once your dry test results in your first sale, you can then put together the program in the weeks (or more likely months) between when you get the contract and the actual speaking date.

Trainer Gary Blake and I did this with "Interpersonal Skills for IS Professionals." We created a letter and dry-tested it to 200 names. Only when we got a company to hire us did we develop the actual program. We chose a date seven weeks out to ensure enough time to create the course, design the class materials, and practice. If the dry test bombs and no one hires you, you've saved yourself the considerable time and effort of preparing a seminar no one wants you to give.

Chapter 3

Putting Together
Your Program

Blondie: You've been working for hours, honey . . . what is it you're doing?

Dagwood: I'm writing a very important speech I have to make tomorrow.

Blondie: What have you written so far?

Dagwood: "Good morning ladies and gentlemen" . . . and I'm not too sure I'll use that.

There's an old saying that experts don't know more than others, but their information is better organized. Speakers are experts who deliver their information via the platform. The more organized your information, the more effective your presentation.

The four steps to creating a presentation are (1) deciding on your topic, (2) research, (3) organizing the information, and (4) writing the talk. Of these, (3) is by far the most critical. Most speakers are already voracious readers on their topics of interest, with no shortage of material at hand. As for writing, if you aren't already a clear, decent writer, you can learn to become reasonably proficient or hire someone to help you.

But knowing how to organize an effective presentation is the key to success. If the information isn't organized in a sensible scheme, people will have difficulty following your talk. It will be less memorable. And the audience will not learn as much from a random presentation of facts as they would from a cohesive, unified lecture.

Here are some ways to organize information for effective presentation:

✔ **Order of location.** A lecture on the planets of the solar system might begin with Mercury (the planet nearest the sun) and end with Pluto (the planet farthest out).

✔ **Order of increasing difficulty.** Computer manuals often start with the easiest material and, as the users master basic principles, move on to more complex operations.

✔ **Alphabetical order.** This is a logical way to arrange a slide show on vitamins (A, B_6, B_{12}, C, D, E, and so on) or a directory of company employees.

✔ **Chronological order.** Here you present the facts in the order in which they happened. History books are organized this way. So are many case histories, feature stories, corporate biographies, and lectures, especially dealing with expeditions and adventures.

✔ **Problem/solution.** Another format appropriate to case histories and many types of reports, the problem/solution organizational scheme begins with "Here's what the problem was" and continues with "Here's how we solved it."

✔ **Inverted pyramid.** This is the newspaper style of news reporting where the lead paragraph summarizes the story and the following paragraphs present the facts in order of decreasing importance. You can use this format in journal articles, letters, memos, reports, and executive briefings.

✔ **Deductive order.** You can start with a generalization, then support it with particulars. Scientists use this format in research papers that begin with the findings and then state the supporting evidence.

✔ **Inductive order.** Another approach is to begin with specific instances, and then lead the reader to the idea or general principles the instances suggest. This is an excellent way to approach trade journal feature stories.

✔ **List.** The sidebar you're now reading is a list. It describes, in list form, the most common ways to organize information. A seminar for engineers might be titled "Six Tips for Designing Wet Scrubbers" or "Seven Ways to Reduce Your Plant's Electric Bill."

SEMINAR MISSION STATEMENT

The first step in designing a speech or seminar is to define the topic. I do this by writing a "seminar mission statement." This is a short description that says what the topic is, who the audience is, and what the program is supposed to teach them.

By reading just this mission statement, prospective attendees should get a clear picture of what will be covered and why they should attend. Once you have written this paragraph, you can use it as the lead in marketing materials promoting the seminar. You can also send it to meeting sponsors who request a short synopsis of what your program is about. They will probably use this paragraph in promotional materials or conference notebooks describing the various programs they are offering.

Figure 3.1 shows a seminar mission statement I wrote for one of my programs on how to use the Internet as a direct mail medium. Note that it identifies (1) the topic, (2) the audience, (3) what is covered, and (4) the benefits of attending.

Take a moment to write down your topic and craft a seminar mission statement paragraph. Be sure to include a clear explanation of the topic for those who are not familiar with it, as well as specific reasons why the person reading the mission statement would want to spend his or her time and money attending the session.

Doing Direct Mail on the Internet

This program is for marketers who want to start or jump-start their Internet direct mail efforts. If you do not know how to do Internet direct mail, we will show you step-by-step exactly what you must do to write your message, select your e-mail lists, send the message, and generate quality responses without getting flamed. If you already do direct mail on the Internet, we'll show you how to improve results while avoiding mistakes that can cost you sales, customer goodwill, or even your account with your ISP (Internet service provider). You will learn how to plan, create, and implement e-campaigns that generate 5 to 20 percent or greater response rate at a fraction of the cost of traditional direct mail.

FIGURE 3.1 Sample seminar mission statement.

Topic: _____.

Audience: _____.

Description: _____

_____

_____

Benefits to attendees: _____

_____.

Done? Good. You have already completed the first step in putting your speech or seminar together. Many speakers have multiple programs, so you can repeat this process for each program you create.

CHECKLIST APPROACH TO SPEECH DESIGN

For a short speech or lecture, anywhere from a half hour to an hour and a half, you can use the list approach to organize your talk.

Just make a list of the key points or messages you want to cover in your presentation. Then organize your presentation around those points.

Sometimes the content and objective suggest an organizational scheme or hierarchy. For instance, if you are speaking about putting your small business on the Internet, you might start with an overview of the Internet and reasons why small businesses should be on it. Next you might cover selecting and reserving a domain name. Then you could move to writing site content, design, and programming. Finally you might cover more advanced topics such as doing e-commerce on your site.

Other times there is no logical order and the points can be presented in any sequence. This was the approach I used for a recent speech on how to succeed as a freelancer. The outline for this talk is shown in Figure 3.2, which is a reproduction of the actual handout I gave to attendees.

The list approach may seem too simple, but simple solutions are usually the best solutions. Yes, I could have grouped my tips on freelance success by subcategory, perhaps—selling, customer service, time management—but would that make the material any clearer to the listener? In a long print document, maybe. But in a short oral presentation, attempting to convey that organizational hierarchy would only confuse the listener. Lists are easy to write, easy to communicate, and easy to understand. It's a win-win situation for you and your attendees.

Figure 3.3 is a seminar description I provided to a local YMCA that

The 10 Ultimate Secrets of Freelance Success

1. Create, test, and refine a Lead-Generating Machine. Choices: direct mail, telemarketing (cold calling), Internet direct mail.

2. Systematize, customize, automate, and speed Inquiry Fulfillment as much as is humanly possible. A Web site is the ideal mechanism for this. See www.bly.com.

3. Use the Question Approach in Follow-Up. Focus on their problems, and away from your portfolio. Use the conversation to assess requirements and position you and the prospect to move to the next step—and a firm assignment.

4. Use Mind Reading to determine the prospect's budget. Have standard pricing, but make the quote fall within the budget. Offer multiple options (Good, Better, Best) and let the prospect select.

5. Create a system for Following Up those prospects who do not close immediately. Use the FIT formula. Use the Diamond, Gold, Copper ranking method.

6. The ultimate secret to getting repeat business is: _____.

7. The ultimate secret to getting referrals is: _____.

8. Create a system to keep your name in front of prospects and clients. Methods: newsletters, e-zines, clip-and-send, postcards.

9. Minimize competition. Strategies: niching, task specialization, industry specialization, target markets, knowledge, customer service levels, service offerings, guruing, differentiation, attitude, technology.

10. Keep the pipeline filled. Method: statistical probability.

No matter what a man's vocation or avocation may be, the nature of his progress through life is largely dependent upon his ability to sell.

—Frederick W. Nichol

FIGURE 3.2 Outline for a one-hour speech.

wanted me to do a half-day program on how to write a book and get it published. It was sufficient to convince the program director to hire me to do the seminar. I keep a separate file for each of my seminars in Word on my PC, and you should, too. That way you can immediately fax or e-mail them whenever someone asks, "Do you have something about your program in writing?" The quicker you comply with this request, the better your chances of getting hired. If you have to write a document from

> ### How to Write a Nonfiction Book and Get It Published
>
> *Learning Objective:*
>
> This program teaches you how to come up with a marketable idea for a nonfiction book, write the book, and sell it to a major New York publishing house for a $5,000 to $15,000 advance.
>
> *Who Should Attend:*
>
> ✔ Writers.
>
> ✔ Editors.
>
> ✔ Speakers and seminar leaders.
>
> ✔ Professionals.
>
> ✔ Anyone interested in writing and publishing a book.
>
> *Topics Covered:*
>
> ✔ Overview of the book publishing industry today.
>
> ✔ Ten ways to generate ideas for books.
>
> ✔ How to determine whether a publisher would be interested in publishing your book.
>
> ✔ Writing a winning book proposal.
>
> ✔ Getting a good literary agent to represent you.
>
> ✔ Approaching publishers.
>
> ✔ Negotiating the deal.
>
> ✔ Advances and royalties.
>
> ✔ Book contracts.
>
> ✔ Researching and writing the book.
>
> ✔ Pros and cons of traditional publishing vs. self-publishing.

FIGURE 3.3 Seminar description for a half-day program.

scratch every time you get asked for information, your response will be slow and you'll miss out on opportunities.

MODULAR APPROACH TO SEMINAR DESIGN

The list approach works best for shorter programs ranging from a half hour to about 90 minutes. Beyond that, you have to make your seminar a bit more structured, for several reasons.

First, in a short program, you don't need a lot of variety: The attendees can listen to you speak for a straight hour without your losing their attention. Beyond an hour or so, however, their senses need to be engaged in different ways: small groups, exercises, interactive participation, games, workbooks, and so on. These activities must be developed and worked into the program. You need a structured presentation to know when to use these activities and how they help get your training ideas across to the attendees.

Second, not every group has the same interests. By breaking your program up into modules, you can enable clients to customize a course for their group: They can emphasize some modules, while deemphasizing or even eliminating others altogether. Several times I have had a client ask for a full day of training on a single module from a larger program. Without a modular course structure, the availability of this material would have been less apparent to them.

The course content outline for a modular seminar looks very much like the table of contents for a book on the same topic. The major topics, which are the chapter headings of the book, are the module headings in the course outline.

Both book chapters and seminar modules are broken down further into subtopics. I usually have four to six or so subtopics per module. The modular content outline for my seminar "Effective Business Writing" is shown in Figure 3.4.

If a module lasts an hour and I have five topics, I can devote about 10 minutes or so to each topic. Some modules may have more topics, which means I have to cover a list of items in more rapid-fire fashion. If any module gets to more than a dozen submodules, you may want to consider breaking it up into two separate modules.

To create the modules and submodules, write down all the topics, large and small, that you are going to cover in your talk on three-by-five-inch index cards, one topic per card. For a seminar on e-business, these might include topics as broad as "The future of e-business" and as narrow as "How many links should you have per Web page?"

I usually have anywhere from six to eight modules in a full-day seminar. If you plan on having six modules and your class lasts six hours, you can schedule one module per hour. That's a convenience for you, since it's easiest to keep track of time in hour increments. If you had seven modules instead, you'd have to switch to a new one every 51 minutes and 25 seconds, which is a little harder to time!

Effective Business Writing

Module 1: Elements of Business Writing
✔ What is "business writing"?
✔ The six characteristics of good business writing.
✔ Tasks of the business writer:
Letters.
Memos.
Proposals.
Reports.
Articles.
Speeches.
Audiovisual presentations.

Module 2: Fundamentals of Grammar
✔ Key grammatical rules for business writers.
✔ Proper use of punctuation marks.
✔ Guidelines for using abbreviations in business writing.
✔ Guidelines for capitalization.
✔ Basic spelling rules.

Module 3: Principles of Composition
✔ Use of active vs. passive voice.
✔ Use of simple vs. complex language.
✔ How to write more concisely.
✔ Use of specific and concrete terms vs. vague, general language.
✔ Making writing more powerful with visual description.
✔ Rules for handling tenses.
✔ Making writing more readable by keeping sections, paragraphs, and sentences short.
✔ How to keep ideas parallel.
✔ Informal vs. formal, corporate vs. conversational—which style is best?

Module 4: Use of Words and Phrases
✔ Why you should substitute small words for big words.
✔ How to eliminate wordy phrases and redundancies from your writing.
✔ Why you should avoid clichés, corporatese, and overblown phrases.
✔ Misused and troublesome words and phrases.
✔ How to avoid sexist language.
✔ How to achieve a contemporary style.

FIGURE 3.4　Seminar content outline for a full-day program.

Module 5: Principles of Organization
- ✔ How to organize your material to suit the reader's needs.
- ✔ Nine ways to organize a business document for easy reading.
- ✔ Use and misuse of executive summaries, leads, and warm-up paragraphs.
- ✔ How to separate fact from opinion in your writing.
- ✔ Use of headings and subheads to organize business documents.

Module 6: Principles of Communication and Persuasion
- ✔ Five steps to more persuasive writing.
- ✔ How to gain your reader's attention in the first paragraph.
- ✔ Use of facts, opinions, and statistics to prove your case.
- ✔ How to determine when you are giving too much detail.
- ✔ How to get the reader on your side.
- ✔ How to get the reader to take the next step.

Module 7: Principles of Tone
- ✔ Why you should prefer informal to formal language.
- ✔ The Conversation Test.
- ✔ The Breath Test.
- ✔ Use of positive vs. negative words.
- ✔ How to change the reader's behavior or attitude.
- ✔ How to let your personality shine through in your writing.
- ✔ Rules for using contractions in business writing.

Module 8: Special Concerns of the Corporate Writer
- ✔ How to quickly gain specialized background knowledge.
- ✔ The collaboration between the writer and the client/expert—who does what?
- ✔ How to write effectively within the guidelines determined by your supervisor or corporate style guide.
- ✔ What to do if the subject matter is too technical for you to understand.
- ✔ What to do if managers you must work with or interview are uncooperative, arrogant, or poor communicators.
- ✔ Tips for making a boring topic more exciting.
- ✔ How to write for a specific audience.

FIGURE 3.4 *(Continued)*

You can start just by dredging your brain for the information it already contains on the subject. You'll be surprised at how many cards you fill (remember, one topic per card) just from your own knowledge. But don't stop there. Go to the library, take out all the books available on the topic, and check your list against their tables of contents, to make sure you don't leave anything out.

When you're done, go through the cards. Make the cards with big or important topics your main module headings. All other cards that relate to that topic should be placed under that heading as subtopics. Then type out your cards on the computer to make the first draft of the seminar outline. From there, refine until you are satisfied.

RESEARCHING THE INFORMATION

In Chapter 1, I gave the opinion that seminar leaders should not merely be talented speakers but should have genuine, expert-based knowledge of their fields.

If you are "merely a speaker" and presenting someone else's seminar, you may be able to get away with not becoming a research maven. But if you are a subject matter expert, ongoing research will be a vital part of your professional life from today until the day you retire.

Teaching you how to do research is beyond the scope of this book, but a few observations may help.

First, you absolutely must be Web-enabled and comfortable finding your way around on the Internet. The professional speaker who cannot comfortably surf the Net is not in tune with today's world. There is a wealth of information on your topic already posted on the World Wide Web. Why not learn what others say about your topic? Also, you'd be embarrassed if an attendee mentioned a well-known Web site in your field and you'd never seen it, wouldn't you? Keep your Web skills and knowledge up-to-date.

Second, build your own reference library of books on your topic. Buy and read the new, important books on the subject. Keep them organized for easy reference. Same with journals, magazines, newsletters, and newspapers—scan them for relevant articles, clip articles of interest, and file according to subject matter for future reference. Good speakers are well-read.

Third, practice what you preach; stay active in your field or profession. I teach direct marketing and feel confident when I speak because I write dozens of direct marketing promotions a year. If you quit your field to become a full-time speaker, you risk growing stale, irrelevant, and out of touch.

> Be state-of-the-art. Do constant research to keep your knowledge, skills, and information current. Clients want speakers to be ahead of the learning curve, not at the rear. Give them today's best practices, not old saws lifted from decades-old books.

Fourth, put your powers of observation to work for you. Go to conventions, seminars, trade shows, professional meetings. Network with colleagues. Watch people in stores, on the street, at parties or PTA meetings. An alert speaker can observe many incidents that can be turned into entertaining anecdotes and relevant examples for talks and seminars.

Fifth, do primary research. Conduct a survey. Write articles and books on your topic, and as part of that work, call up and interview experts. Gather and analyze data to create proprietary information other speakers can't offer.

DESIGNING THE MODULES

The presentation of subtopics within each module should vary from subtopic to subtopic. If everything is presented in the same format, it's monotonous and boring. Vary your presentation to increase learning and keep the audience alert.

There are many methods of presentation. Here are just a few of the ones you can work into your seminar design:

- ✔ *Lecture.* This is straight talking to the audience—the old college approach.
- ✔ *Interactive.* You lead or facilitate a discussion, rather than just lecture. You ask questions and get responses from your audience. The audience discusses and debates among themselves, with you as the leader.
- ✔ *Video.* You show a videotape covering a particular topic, and may follow the tape with a facilitated group discussion.
- ✔ *Exercises.* You give attendees an exercise to do in class, and evaluate it upon completion.
- ✔ *Role play.* Put attendees into different roles and have them act out scenes without a script. Example: In a sales training seminar,

Ruth is the prospect and Jack is the salesperson. They can then reverse roles, if you wish.

✔ *Small group teams.* You break the class into small groups (usually two to three people per group) and have them do exercises in teams. Then each team presents its results.

✔ *Games.* Attendees, individually or in small groups, play a game which you lead. The purpose is either to dramatize a training message or simply to motivate or refresh attendees. Example: One seminar leader challenges small groups to build a bridge out of Tinkertoys in a limited time to teach teamwork and leadership.

✔ *Multimedia.* Your presentation can incorporate audio, computers, overheads, and other media to make learning more visual, interactive, and exciting.

✔ *Busy hands.* Have attendees draw pictures, mold clay into shapes, put a puzzle together, or do another activity that involves their hands. Also desirable is an activity that gets them out of their seats, like Simon Says or simple physical exercise.

When doing longer presentations (half day or more), do not make the entire program straight lecture. People will find it dull. Use modular seminar design to break the program into many short topics, then apply these different training methods to add motion, entertainment, and variety. Remember, if they snooze, you lose.

CLEAR COMMUNICATION

A speaker said, "Learning can occur as a result of feedback from the result of action previously taken or from the contemplation of potential future actions." It's lines like this one that sometime make me ashamed to be in the training business!

The attendee may already be bored just by being forced to sit in a classroom; don't make it worse by trying to talk like a college professor—which, by the way, impresses almost no one. Instead, talk like a person. The attendee will like you better.

I have only a few suggestions for being a speaker people will like to listen to and be able to understand:

1. Talk in plain English. Use technical terms only when necessary and not to impress people. When you use a technical term, explain it clearly so everyone understands.

2. Be yourself. Let your natural personality shine through. The more the attendees can relate to you as a human being, the more receptive to your ideas they'll be.

3. Don't worry about using speaking techniques, such as artificially raising your voice to a shout or lowering it to a whisper for dramatic effect, as some speaking coaches advise. Just be straightforward in your talk and natural in your actions. Be a person, not an entertainer.

AUDIOVISUAL AIDS

"The days are over when you can impress an audience with a few rough overheads and a handful of catchy stories," says Sharon Yoder, director of faculty at CompEd Solutions. "You're standing in front of people accustomed to being visually stimulated and entertained by TV, movies, videos, interactive computers, and all the other emerging technologies that are popping up at record pace."

I have mixed feelings. The top professional speakers rarely use PowerPoint or other computer-based presentations, because the result can be boring and stilted.

Corporate managers and executives, often the worst speakers, are almost wholly reliant on laptops and PowerPoint.

A speaker who has complex visuals has to focus too much attention on the mechanics of the computer or slide projector, which in turn makes him or her less focused on the audience.

I typically give my speeches with no prepared visuals. I request from the sponsor a flip chart on an easel with markers. I may prepare some flip charts in the room before the audience gets there in the morning, then reveal them during the talk by flipping the pages. I also write on the flip charts during the talk. This adds a degree of human interaction that slick, prepared computer graphics cannot match.

But I fear I am losing the battle and may soon have to give in to the computer age. In the corporate market, an increasing number of conferences and meetings put in their speaker requirements that you prepare visual aids in PowerPoint and provide them in advance of your talk. Not having them makes you look uncooperative, and people ask, "Where are your PowerPoint slides?" In the past when I didn't do PowerPoint materials, many people commented after my talk that they were amazed someone could be entertaining and hold attention without computer visuals. But more and more meeting planners require them, and I'm getting tired of fighting the battle.

The good news is: PowerPoint is relatively easy to use. (If I can do it, you can, too.) And, there are plenty of computer artists around who will do your PowerPoint presentations for you at a reasonable price, if you prefer not to learn it yourself.

TRAINING EXERCISES, ACTIVITIES, AND HANDOUTS

I am a big fan of handouts. They can get unwieldy in large crowds. But they work nicely in smaller groups.

For an in-house corporate training class with 10 to 30 students, I use a series of handouts keyed to my various module subtopics. I typically have two to three handouts per module, which is about 20 handouts for a one-day course.

For an association or corporate meeting breakout session with 20 to 50 attendees, I have one handout that serves as the course outline, as shown in Figure 3.2.

If I am doing a keynote (rare for me) to a group of 75 or more, I usually skip the handout or provide a master that the sponsor can duplicate and hand out with the meeting materials.

Some seminar leaders prefer to bind their handouts with a cover and call it a "workbook." Workbooks are convenient to reproduce and ship. You can even charge your client an additional fee per workbook.

Handouts have a lower perceived value, and clients don't expect to pay for them. The advantage, however, is that you can hand them out as the subject arises. With a workbook, everything gets handed out at the beginning. Some attendees will read it immediately, skipping ahead to topics before you're ready to introduce them, and not paying attention to your talk as they read.

Figure 3.5 shows a handout that was distributed at a meeting of our town's Boy Scout and Cub Scout troops. The kids were given the exercise as a way of getting motivated for the meeting and getting to know each other and their leaders. You can see how you could easily

Life is like a roll of film. You take your best shot, but you never know what's going to develop.
                    —*From a radio commercial for Summit Bank*

Human Treasure Hunt

1. **You must find a fellow member of the group who can identify with each box.**
2. **Write the person's name in the box.**
3. **You are allowed to use someone's name only *once*.**
4. **You cannot use your own name.**
5. **If you fill all of the boxes *you win!!!***

Has a cat or dog.	Has been on a cruise.	Has been on TV.	Has been married 10 years.	Uses a PC.
Is a vegetarian.	Has been to California.	Has won money at Atlantic City.	Has children.	Has read a Tom Peters book.
Has own Web site.	Was born on an odd-numbered day.	Has been to Europe.	Has been to a World Series or Super Bowl.	Was born outside the United States.
Speaks a foreign language.	Has been to Long Island.	Has been snow skiing.	Has been to Disney World.	Takes vitamins or herbs.

FIGURE 3.5 Sample training exercise: "Getting to know each other."

adapt this to a corporate training seminar for attendees to get to know one another.

Look for ways to go beyond the ordinary and make your handouts fun and interactive. Not every handout can be special—many will be ordinary checklists and worksheets—but try fresh ideas. What about handing out a blank sheet of paper and seeing which team can make a paper airplane that goes farthest? This could be used in team-building sessions or teaching creative thinking.

Getting Good

A young man gets into a taxicab in New York City and asks the driver, "How do I get to Carnegie Hall?"

"Practice, my boy, practice," the driver answers.

The only way to gain comfort, confidence, and competence as a speaker is by speaking. You cannot listen to a tape, read a book, take a seminar, get an advanced degree in education, absorb the information, and then conclude, "Now I know how to speak!" You would be wrong. Theory is one thing; practice is another. Some skills can be learned only by doing, and that certainly applies to public speaking.

Public speaking is not technical or complex. In fact, the more techniques you read or are told about by speaking coaches, the worse you might actually become! The reason is that if you concentrate on technique, then you are not concentrating on what's really important—the topic and the audience.

I advise you to forget the technique and speak plainly and naturally. If you have a natural sense of humor, using it will give you an advantage. The same for a natural warmth and friendliness. But don't force yourself to be someone you're not. Take what you are and use it. If you are authoritative, be the authority in your field. If you are a genius, dazzle the audience with your sharp thinking and calculated insights.

HAVE A CONVERSATION WITH THE AUDIENCE

The one thing speaking coaches will tell you that I agree with 100 percent is to look individuals in the audience directly in the eye while you talk. As you talk, move from individual to individual, making eye contact with each. That way, you are literally having a conversation with the audience one person at a time, not lecturing before the masses.

"The audience is one person," writes Charles Osgood in his book *Osgood on Speaking* (William Morrow). "Even though you are talking to a number of people, you are talking to them one at a time. That is to say, they are *hearing* you one at a time. Therefore you should *not* pitch your voice as if you were a drill sergeant addressing a platoon or a teacher lecturing a class. You should imagine, just as I do when I'm on radio or television, that you are speaking to an audience of one."

As you normally do when you have a conversation, speak like a human being. One seminar leader actually said in a class, "Decisions are the transform between knowledge and action." When I heard this, I moaned silently. What is a "transform"? In what way does this statement make clearer the concept of decision making? Sociologist Susan Brownmiller defines jargon as, "Language more complex than the subject it serves to communicate," and this is a perfect example. Don't use jargon. (I almost wrote "Eschew jargon," but quickly realized "eschew" means "don't use," and simple language is always the best language.) Use simple language. Talk in plain English.

As in regular conversations, talk. Use notes, visuals, and handouts— or perhaps an outline—to guide your conversation and show you what topic you should be on next. But use the notes as guidelines only. Speak from the experience and knowledge in your brain; don't recite a written treatise. In his book *The Toastmaster's Manual* (Droke), Harold W. Donahue writes:

> Reading from manuscript is one of the prime reasons for inadequate or inaccurate study of your audience. Now and then you will find a man who can read and observe his audience more or less simultaneously. But such skill is acquired only after long practice. Most of us would never become very proficient. We are so occupied with the words on a printed page that we can think of little else. And the man who is giving a canned talk from memory is not in a much more favorable position. He is concentrating every effort on *remembering*. The audience becomes not a group of normal human beings, but merely something to speak to.
>
> Thus you readily see that the man who speaks extemporaneously, or who uses notes memorizing *ideas* rather than actual words, has a marked advantage. His talk is more plastic, and he can experiment until he finds himself in rhythm with the audience.

The audience wants to share not only your knowledge but your wit, your mind, even the way you think. They also want your *current* thinking on your subject, including new stories and the latest developments. I like to tell my audience something that happened to me personally or professionally—or both—that very week, if possible. That shows my presentation is fresh and hasn't grown stale "in the can."

PRACTICING

According to a bulletin from the Boxlight Corporation titled *Presentation Power*, "Well-rehearsed presentations become less scripted and mechanical in delivery and more conversational."

The more you give a particular presentation, the more comfortable and effective you'll become at giving it. Simple as that.

The first time you give a presentation is never the best time. You get better as you go along. That's why I urge speakers who make videos and audiotapes as demos and products to rerecord them every year or so. You're much better today than you were 12 months ago, but the year-old tapes feature you back then, not now. So they do not present you at your best.

Can you do a dry run before the actual performance? You can try. But I find that without a live audience in front of me, a dry run in my office or the empty seminar room before the attendees arrive isn't effective preparation or training for me. I need the audience and their reactions to gauge whether my talk is working. Talking to myself in a room just doesn't cut it. You may have a similar reaction.

How can you get real experience giving your speech to a live audience before you are at the point where people will hire you? Offer to give your talk for free to any group who will have you. You want experience, not pay. (Of course there are other benefits you can get from the free talk, including referrals, leads from prospects sitting in the audience, testimonials from attendees and sponsors, and maybe an audiotape or a videotape of the presentation you can turn into a demo or sell as an information product.)

WORKING WITH A COACH

By now you know this book is highly opinionated, reflecting my strong personal biases in terms of a certain style and approach to professional speaking.

Many speaking defects can be overcome just by slowing down and speaking up. Two of the most common reasons for being difficult to understand are talking too fast and not speaking loud enough. What's the right speed? In his book *Public Speaking As Listeners Like It* (Harper & Brothers), Richard C. Borden advises a speaking rate of 90 to 160 words a minute. Vary your speed within this range and modulate your volume naturally from soft to loud, so that your speech is not monotonous.

Perhaps hiring a speaking coach will help you gain confidence, overcome stage fright, and be a better presenter. If you believe so, by all means try it. You have nothing to lose but your time and the coaching fee.

My experience is that most speaking coaches who train would-be professional speakers put too much emphasis on theatrics and dramatics, encouraging a phony, show-business type platform persona. I would advise you to seek a coach who specializes in training corporate executives rather than professional speakers, with an emphasis on clear oral communication rather than showmanship.

PRESENTATION TIPS

Dr. Rob Gilbert is one of the country's top motivational speakers and a master of teaching presentation skills to others. At the beginning of a recent Gilbert workshop I attended on "How to Give a Speech," Dr. Gilbert told his audience: "If you get one good idea from this session, it will have been worth the price." In fact, I got at least 42 good ideas on improving presentation skills, and Dr. Gilbert has generously given permission for me to share them with you.

1. Write your own introduction and mail it to the sponsoring organization in advance of your appearance.
2. Establish rapport with the audience early.
3. What you say is not as important as how you say it.
4. Self-effacing humor works best.
5. Ask the audience questions.
6. Don't give a talk—have a conversation.

If you have certain bad habits in speaking, such as saying "you know" or keeping your hands in your pockets, videotape yourself and then watch and listen to the tape. It will make you painfully aware of how these tics, which seem minor to you while you are speaking, detract from your platform presence and performance. Make a short (10-minute) training tape consisting of nothing but you exhibiting these tics and watch it before each new performance. Seeing yourself stumble will do more to make you conscious of any problems and help you avoid them than any instructor can.

7. Thirty percent of the people in the audience will never ask the speaker a question.

8. A little bit of nervous tension is probably good for you.

9. Extremely nervous? Use rapport building, not stress reduction, techniques.

10. The presentation does not have to be great. Tell your audience that if they get one good idea out of your talk, it will have been worthwhile for them.

11. People want stories, not information.

12. Get the audience involved.

13. People pay more for entertainment than education. (Proof: The average college professor would have to work 10 centuries to earn what Oprah Winfrey makes in a year.)

14. You have to love what you are doing. (Dr. Gilbert has 8,000 cassette tapes of speeches and listens to these tapes three to four hours a day.)

15. The first time you give a particular talk it will not be great.

16. The three hardest audiences to address: engineers, accountants, and high school students.

17. If heckled, you can turn any situation around ("verbal aikido").

18. Communicate from the Heart + Have an Important Message = Speaking Success.

19. You can't please everybody, so don't even try. Some will like you and your presentation and some won't.

20. Ask your audience how you are doing and what they need to hear from you to rate you higher.

21. Be flexible. Play off your audience.

22. Be totally authentic.

23. To announce a break say: "We'll take a five-minute break now, so I'll expect you back here in ten minutes." It always gets a laugh.

24. To get them back in the room (if you are the speaker), go out into the hall and shout, "He's starting; he's starting!"

25. Courage is to feel the fear and do it anyway. The only way to overcome what you fear is to do it.

26. If panic strikes: Just give the talk and keep your mouth moving. The fear will subside in a minute or two.

27. In speaking, everything you see, read, hear, do, or experience is grist for the mill.

28. Tell touching stories.

29. If the stories are about you, be the goat, not the hero. People like speakers who are humble; audiences hate bragging and braggarts.

30. Join Toastmasters. Take a Dale Carnegie course in public speaking. Join the National Speakers Association.

31. Go hear the great speakers and learn from them.

32. If you borrow stories or techniques from other speakers, adapt this material and use it in your own unique way.

33. Use audiovisual aids if you wish, but not as a crutch.

34. When presenting a daylong workshop, make the afternoon shorter than the morning.

35. Asking people to perform a simple physical exercise (stretching, Simon Says, etc.) as an activity during a break can increase their energy level and overcome lethargy.

36. People love storytellers.

37. Today's most popular speaking topic: change (in business, society, lifestyles, etc.) and how to cope with it.

38. There is no failure—just feedback.

39. At the conclusion of your talk, tell your audience that they were a great audience even if they were not.

40. Ask for applause using this closing: "You've been a wonderful audience. [*Pause*] Thank you very much."

41. If you want to become a good speaker, give as many talks as you can to as many groups as you can, even if you don't get paid at first. You will improve as you gain experience. (Dr. Gilbert has some speeches he has given more than 1,000 times.)

42. Cruise lines frequently offer speakers free trips in exchange for a brief lecture during the cruise. And they do not demand top, experienced speakers.

GOING TO THE NEXT LEVEL

The best way to get paid big money as a speaker and consultant, other than to become a celebrity or write a best-selling book, is to be as good as you can, continually strive to get even better, and deliver to clients more than they have a right to expect.

Speaker Mikki Williams observes: "The mediocre speaker tells; the good speaker explains; the superior speaker demonstrates; the great speaker inspires."

"It's not enough to present information," says speaker Rob Gilbert. "You have to give your audience hope."

Add value to your presentations. Give the audience—and the client who hired you—something extra. Speaker Joyce Gioia gives the following suggestions for adding value to your talk:

✔ If speaking at a trade show, highlight exhibitors' products and services in your program.

✔ Get the local press to cover the event.

✔ In advance, call three people you know will be in the audience and weave their comments into your talk. Then in the talk you can say, "Joe had a good idea" or "Rick found this to be true when he computerized his payroll." Doing so establishes a connection with the group (and especially the individual) and helps convince them that you have done your homework and taken the time to understand the quirks of their particular industry or business.

✔ Use a crossword puzzle to reinforce learning. Parsons Software (800-PARSONS) has an inexpensive program, CrossWords Plus 2.0, you can use to create your own custom crossword puzzles quickly and easily.

✔ Find a sponsor willing to contribute money toward your fee or gifts to be used as door prizes.

Here is a standard opening given to me by Rob Gilbert. I have used it dozens of times with success. You can substitute the name of your client or sponsor for "John," your topic for "Topic X," and the name of your client for "ABC Organization." Or, create your own standard opening. It's up to you.

> When John was looking for a speaker, he called the speaker he knew who was the most experienced in Topic X, explained about this meeting of ABC Organization, and asked him to present. He said, "I'm sorry, but I can't."
>
> John decided that if he couldn't get the most experienced expert in Topic X, he would get the person who was the best speaker. But when he called, that person said, "I'm sorry, but I can't."
>
> "I couldn't get the most expert or the best presenter," John said to himself, "so I'll just get the speaker on Topic X who is the best looking." But when John called, that person said he could not give the talk.
>
> A few weeks ago, I got a call from John asking if I could speak on Topic X at this meeting of ABC Organization. I thought, "I can't say 'no' to this guy four times in a row. . . ." So here I am.

✔ Find something from that day's news and incorporate it into your message.

✔ Publicly acknowledge the meeting planner or president of the organization. Find a way to relate the acknowledgment to your topic.

✔ Ask the meeting planner what you could do (that you're not already doing) to make his or her life easier and less stressful.

✔ Be flexible. If they need you to speak for more or less time than expected, do so graciously.

✔ Give away a reminder list of the highlights of your speech.

Develop a standard opening of one to three minutes and memorize it. This way, you can begin on familiar ground and concentrate on the audience, not your material. Once you establish this easy atmosphere, you can work from notes rather than a written script or memorized speech.

MORE SPEAKING TIPS

My colleague James Obermayer, himself a professional speaker, was called upon to coach executives at a corporation on how to be more effective public speakers. Here is the advice he gave them (reprinted with his permission, of course):

1. *Arrive early.* Show up in your presentation room at least 15 minutes early to test the sound system, computer connection, lighting, and placement of the podium and flip chart.

2. *Test the equipment before everyone shows up.* Test the sound and projection systems before the first attendees arrive. Know where the microphone has to be placed, near you on the podium. The first they hear from you shouldn't be the infamous "Testing, testing."

3. *Check and adjust the lighting.* Make sure that overhead lights in the room are not washing out the projection screen. Take the bulbs out above the screen or tone back the lights. Try to avoid standing in a darkened area—the audience likes to see the speaker.

4. *The introduction.* Make sure the person who introduces you can do an adequate job by providing a brief introduction written for the occasion. It should be no more than 50 words. If the person has written an intro he or she wants to use, great. But, there is nothing worse than the introducer starting off by saying, "I don't know who this person is, although I hear she is very good."

5. *Start and finish on time.* Your audience expects to hear your entire presentation. If you don't start on time you will probably finish late. If you are pressed for time, you may be tempted to skip over material. The audience feels cheated if you say, "Oh, the stuff is in here—read it later." They came to hear you and not read it later. It is discourteous to finish late.

6. *Create your own beginning.* Aside from an opening that could be humorous (but don't do it if you're not comfortable with it),

or a story that leads you into the reason why you're there, make sure that if the introduction was skimpy you fill it in with a short autobiography. Then tell the audience what they will learn; just list the six or eight high points. (More about the adult learning model later.)

7. *Opening?* Stories that make a point are good openers. It doesn't always have to be humor. Jim says he sometimes starts off presentations with a simple question such as: "Who said, 'Toto, I don't think we're in Kansas anymore?'" A dozen hands jump in the air, and the presentation is off to a good start. Jim tells them yes, Dorothy said it in *The Wizard of Oz*, and then he connects it to today's changing business environment. The presentation starts when you utter your first word to the audience, not when you say "Testing, testing."

8. *Have fun!* Listeners like speakers who are having fun. Smile, and laugh at mistakes. Don't take yourself so seriously.

9. *Speak to audience members before you start.* Ask why they are there—what interested them in attending. It can often give you stories to tell. You'll also find you're more relaxed when you do start.

10. *Use the adult learning model.* Tell them what you're going to tell them, tell them, and tell them what you've told them.

11. *What if you make a mistake?* So what. Flub a line, mispronounce a word? Laugh about it and move on. People don't care, and they have empathy.

12. *Special PowerPoint Tip.* While the slides are on the screen, if you want to go to a black screen touch "b" on the keyboard and the screen will go to black. Touch "w" and it will go to white. This is especially helpful when you have a point to make that takes time and you want people to stop reading the slide for the nth time and focus on what you, the speaker, are saying.

13. *Never speak to the screen.* You can refer to the screen and point to the screen, but speak to the audience, not the screen. The screen isn't your audience.

14. *Talk to the audience, one at a time.* There are a lot of techniques about involving the audience and not just talking to your notes (or the screen). One good technique is to talk to different peo-

ple at different times. Pick a person and talk to him or her for 30 seconds. Pick another one and move on.

15. *Slides are not for you to read.* Your audience can read the slides; you don't have to do it for them. Use the slides as talking points. Avoid reading every word. Pick and choose what's on the screen. Paraphrase.

16. *Using notes?* Avoid using lengthy notes. Simple three-by-five-inch cards with main talking points are all that are needed to keep you on track.

17. *Rehearse.* Rehearse the presentation at least five times. Read the material on the slides and overheads out loud, and you'll get to know it well enough that you won't have to read it. You'll know it, and the audience will know that you know it.

18. *Handouts or not?* Handouts are good for workshops and seminars. They are a tangible take-away. Give them out beforehand. Use the "Header and Footer" portion under "View" in Power-Point to add your company name, phone number, and copyright. The presentation may be photocopied later and with your name and phone number you have increased visibility for many years to come.

19. *Empty your pockets.* If you start with empty pockets you won't be inclined to rattle change and make noise during your speech. The audience is easily distracted. Their minds move faster than your slides or your speech, so any distractions are easily noticed.

20. *Don't forget water.* In just a one-hour speech, you can expel as much as a quart of water. Have water handy on the podium and use it.

21. *Allow for questions.* Leave about five minutes at the end for questions.

22. *How do you handle questions from the audience?* Repeat the question from the audience. If possible, ask the person's name and company, and repeat it to the audience. People love hearing their names. Plus, you like to know who you're talking to.

23. *Difficult questions from the audience?* If a difficult question takes you off guard you can: (1) Turn it around on the audience and see if someone else has an answer. If the person is a heckler, others in the audience will often disagree and put the per-

son in his or her place. Look for people shaking their heads in disgust and call on them—they will usually defend you better than you can defend yourself. (2) Say you'll get an answer for the questioner later. Ask for his or her business card. (3) Refer the question to a qualified person from the company who is also in the presentation. "George, would you like to handle that for me?"

24. *Use timing cards.* If you have a friend in the audience, make up three timing notices, each on a separate sheet of paper. The first one should read "30 minutes" and be shown at 30 minutes, the second at 45 minutes, and the third at 5 minutes prior to the finish for a typical one-hour presentation. The friend should flash the timing cards to you to let you know where you stand. Don't ignore them or wave back.

25. *Recap in closing.* Recap the high points of your speech. List the four to six things you want people to remember. Tell them what you've told them.

26. *Share your last slide.* List your name, company, phone number, and Web site at the end of the presentation on the last slide. Leave it up while you're answering questions.

27. *Rehearse, again and again.* One more time: The single greatest contributor to a good presentation is rehearsal. Do yourself a favor and go over your presentation again and again. You'll be a better presenter and enjoy yourself more.

28. *Have fun.* This bears repeating. Listeners like people who are having fun. Smile, and laugh at mistakes. Seriously, don't take yourself too seriously.

ON THE DAY OF THE SEMINAR . . .

The day of the big presentation has finally arrived. Everyone will be there—your client, your next potential client, and, who knows, maybe even your mother. The stakes are high for your budding speaking career: You need a good performance, good ratings from the audience, a testimonial and referral from the client, and a good tape to turn into a product or demo. You've practiced your presentation so many times you can do it in your sleep. You arrive at the airport, dash to the hotel, and finally walk into the hotel meeting room an hour before you're to deliver the pitch—but it's not at all like you expected. The best presentation efforts can be derailed by room setup variables that are unanticipated. Next time you're dashing to an off-site meeting, consider these key elements.

How Controllable Is the Lighting?

In many hotel settings, each room has a number of different configurations based on the specific needs of the group. First check out where your lighting controls are located. Dimmer switches are ideal, allowing you to dim the ambient light to the point that makes your colors crisp and bright on-screen but not so dark that your audience is tempted to get caught up on their jet lag. It is best to be able to control the lighting directly above the screen in order to get the best image.

Sound Support

Balancing sound in a hotel meeting room will take some trial and error. An unnaturally amplified voice can take what could have been a personal presentation and give it a large impersonal auditorium feel.

Use a cordless lapel microphone whenever possible to give you the freedom to move around the room without having to worry about an umbilical cord. Once you've established a good volume level, consider how you will be supporting the sound elements that might be coming from your laptop computer. Whether they're voice-overs, music, or appropriate sound effects, they will not carry adequately from the small laptop speakers. The house or room sound systems may adequately handle the sound, but you might want to run the sound into your electronic projector and test its adequacy to support the room size.

If your projector has external audio capabilities, familiarize yourself, via a phone call to the hotel, with what you need for connections to use the house speaker system. This call will ensure that you are prepared with the correct cabling and connectors if you decide to use the house system.

Seating and Platform Support

Seating can be a critical element in creating a speaker-focused room environment. Project your image to fill the screen and then spend a few minutes walking around the seats. Is the line of sight impaired or are chairs placed too far to the edges to see your projected visuals? Now is the time to take care of this with the hotel staff. Check with the meeting host to determine needs of the other presenters, and set up the room so it works well for them but also make sure it is optimum for your objectives. For those presenters who like to be more mobile, the ability to create a middle aisle and close the distance with your audience from time to time can be an effective technique. As you move into the aisle and close the gap, attention levels will rise in the audience.

Having an elevated platform can often provide a greater degree of visibility to a larger room full of people. In smaller settings, elevated platforms can have an unintended effect. The increased distance creates an awkward space that impairs the ability to connect with your audience. You become a distant talking head, making it nearly impossible to create strong impressions.

What's Going on Nearby?

Because of the catering services offered by many hotels, the kitchen and dish rooms are often right off the meeting room itself. Many a presentation has been disrupted by the sounds of clanging dishes and boisterous support staff. Checking on what activities will be occurring in a nearby kitchen, before your meeting, may save a great deal of frustration later. Also, determine when other meetings will be breaking up around your meeting room. The stampede of human bodies from adjoining rooms will compete for the attention of your audience during critical parts of a presentation.

There are many ways to adequately prepare for a presentation. We generally think in terms of creating crisp messages and nicely constructed graphics, but don't forget the room. When the stakes are high and your tolerance for last-minute snafus is low, a call ahead for room layout can mean the difference between starting the big presentation frazzled or being in confident control.

The key to achieving success, regardless of your occupation, is determination. You must have the attitude that no matter what obstacles may come your way, nothing will stop you from being successful. If you have that mindset, luck usually follows.
—Chaunce Hayden, editor, *Steppin' Out* magazine

Don't miss these often overlooked tips:

✔ Check out the podium before the presentation. Adjust the height and distance to the audience to ensure you can be seen and can easily move about.

✔ Enlist an assistant to help with details like chairs, lighting, sound, seating, and general crowd control.

✔ Fill up the front rows first by taping off the back rows before the attendees arrive.

✔ Make sure the screen is large enough to be seen by all. If you're going to be projecting onto a wall, make sure it's a light color with no texture to distort your presentation.

Chapter

Market Opportunity #1: Keynotes and Breakouts

People love meetings—planning and attending them at least, if not actually listening to the speaker. In his book *How to Manage Your Meetings* (Drake House Publishers), Harold Donahue observes:

> There will always be meetings—there always have been meetings. Some of the oldest records of the human family tell of gatherings to honor a victorious hunter, or to plan a strategy of war. Holy Writ is essentially a continuing story of people in unison. Again and again, we find groups meeting, talking, acting together. Jesus Christ spent His entire adult life conducting meetings. Only thus could He hope to spread His simple story of salvation to a waiting world.

Meetings can range from informal workplace get-togethers among a few colleagues to large, formal affairs attended by thousands. The larger the meeting, the better the chance that the meeting planner will hire paid speakers.

There are two types of presentations paid speakers give: keynote and breakout. The keynote is usually the main speech of the entire event, or at least of a given day of the event (although sometimes there are separate keynotes at each meal). All or at least a large percentage of the audience attends the keynote, and there are usually no other sessions being held during the same time period. The keynote presentations usually pay top dollar when paid speakers are used.

Breakouts are sessions held throughout the day. Often there are two, three, or more breakouts being held concurrently, and the audience members choose which they want to attend. Some go to yours; others choose different topics. So the attendance at each breakout is smaller than at the keynote, because you pull only a fraction of the audience (also, some attendees skip breakouts to play golf or relax at the facility).

The common element of keynotes and breakouts is that they are shorter than public seminars or in-house corporate training seminars. Keynotes and breakouts, whether at association conferences or corporate meetings, average about an hour. Keynotes typically range from 30 to 60 minutes, with breakouts running a bit longer: 60 to 90 minutes.

The presentations at these meetings are speeches more than seminars or workshops. The reason is twofold: the time is short, and the crowds are often large. Therefore, while a good speaker may engage the audience on a limited basis through conversation and perhaps some interactive exercises, the lecture has to have a structure and flow firmly controlled by the speaker: If you try to make the group too loose and informal, chaos will result. Also, the audience is expecting a speech, not a workshop, so they may be resistant to too much activity and interaction. Some just want to sit and listen quietly until it's time for the golf outing or whatever is planned for the afternoon.

A lot of speakers love the meetings marketplace and prefer it to longer formats such as public seminars and corporate training. One reason is that the presentation is more of a performance; the speaker is pressed to entertain the group, as well as inform. Knowing that learning in these short sessions is often limited, some meeting planners put a premium on entertainment, and speakers who emphasize style over substance are only too happy to oblige. When someone tells you, "I want to be a professional speaker," the keynote and breakout sessions at associa-

A *conference* is a multiday meeting featuring multiple speakers and breakout sessions. Conferences may be sponsored by associations or put on by specialized *conference companies* that produce conferences as a business.

tion conferences and corporate meetings are probably what they envision themselves doing.

OVERVIEW OF THE KEYNOTE AND BREAKOUT MARKET

Although it's not always the case, keynotes and breakouts tend to be given by people who consider themselves *professional speakers* rather than trainers or seminar leaders.

Trainers typically present intensive programs to a small group of an organization's employees. Group size ranges from 6 to 30, although it can be higher. Most training sessions are one day; some are half a day, and a smaller percentage are two days or longer.

Professional speakers speak to larger groups, typically ranging from 50 to 50,000. Their venues include rallies, sales meetings, conferences, and association events. Most talks are an hour to 90 minutes. A keynote talk means you are the main speaker of the day. A breakout talk means you are one of a number of speakers giving smaller workshops. If a client invites you to do one session, offer to do multiple sessions. You add value, amortize the cost of your travel and lodging over several talks, and can charge more for the additional sessions.

According to an article in *Sharing Ideas* (January 1998, page 5), the 10 most popular speech topics for sessions at corporate and association meetings are:

1. Motivation.
2. Change.
3. Sales.
4. Team building.
5. The future.
6. Humor.
7. Leadership.
8. Customer service.
9. Big-name speakers.
10. Entertainers.

Authors frequently get calls to give sessions at meetings on their topics. When you write and publish books and articles on a topic, you are

If you speak on topics that are appropriate for a business audience, there are thousands of associations that hire speakers. One good reference source is the *Directory of Association Meeting Planners and Conference/Convention Directors*. Updated annually, the directory lists more than 13,600 association meeting professionals. Listings indicate professional speaker usage as well as size and number of meetings, destinations, lengths, and schedule.

perceived as an expert. Many authors get calls from companies, associations, and schools asking them to conduct programs on the topics of their books. If you want to generate more of these inquiries, include a description of your program, address, and phone number in the bios that run with your articles and books. I got a $6,000 contract from the U.S. government because someone in the Army had found my phone number in the back of my book *The Elements of Business Writing*.

Local groups, and local chapters of national groups, typically pay no fee or a small honorarium. There are exceptions.

National associations pay significant fees to speakers who give talks at national meetings: $1,000 to $3,000 for a talk ranging from an hour to half a day. Sometimes the pay is even better. I know one meeting planner who paid an author $6,000 for a one-hour talk. Best-selling authors like John Naisbitt and Tom Peters can command $10,000 to $40,000 or more per talk, but they are the exception, not the rule. The top fee for non-celebrity speakers is about $5,000.

Is the association and corporate meeting market for you? It depends on your personality and what you enjoy. Many consultants are excellent communicators and teachers, but some are comfortable only when there is a printed page or a telephone line between them and their audience, or they are meeting one or two people in private. If you are introverted and dislike public speaking, you may still be able to make money speaking—but you simply may not want to.

On the other hand, if you are as comfortable at the podium as you are with a cell phone or spreadsheet, consider giving teaching and speaking a try. It's a nice change of pace from the isolation of working at home. So are the fat paychecks—and the applause when you finish.

For more information on speaking at association and corporate meetings, contact the National Speakers Association and American Seminar Leaders Association. Both are listed in Appendix D. Subscribe to *Sharing Ideas* magazine, listed in Appendix A.

WHO HIRES SPEAKERS IN THIS MARKET?

Your potential client is the meeting planner. At national association meetings, this person is often a full-time meeting planner on the association staff. For a corporation, if the meeting is a sales or marketing meeting, the meeting planner may be the manager of sales or of marketing. Associations are more likely to have meeting planners on staff than corporations.

At a corporation, the manager in charge of a particular region or functional area will have overall responsibility for big meetings. He or she in turn may delegate most of the work to an assistant, an outside meeting planner, or both.

Executives at associations and corporations increasingly work on a fast track and in a short time frame, so when they call, it's important to give them fast access to your program descriptions. Keep on your hard drive one file for each seminar, and e-mail it to the executive upon request. Also have all the seminar description files posted on your Web site for viewing and download. A sample description for one of my breakout sessions (I do very little keynote work) is shown in Figure 5.1.

The description has a title, an introductory paragraph of descriptive text, and a list of bullet points indicating what will be covered in the session. Use this format. Reason: The meeting planner is looking for electronic copy he or she can lift word for word from your file and plug into the conference brochure or handouts being developed for the meeting. The more you can supply the materials he or she needs ready-made, the less work the meeting planner has to do.

Meeting planners are incredibly busy and pressed for time. The more effort you put into making their jobs easier, the happier they will be, and the more likely they will be to hire you again.

WORKING IN THE MEETING MARKETPLACE

Because most would-be speakers and professional speakers prefer doing keynotes at big meetings to other venues and formats, the competition here is greater than in any other area of the seminar, training, and workshop business. So, although keynote speakers command top dollar, the

---

Active Listening

This seminar helps people improve their listening skills on the telephone, at meetings, and in one-to-one conversations. The workshop will demonstrate and offer practice in the art of listening, showing people how to overcome bad listening habits, improve body language, understand their listening styles, and gain empathy with coworkers and customers.

Objectives

✔ Learn to identify the three levels of listening.

✔ Understand the need for improved listening skills.

✔ Overcome bad listening habits.

✔ Improve body language.

✔ Understand your individual listening style.

✔ Understand the principles of active listening.

✔ Learn to recognize distractions to listening.

✔ Use active listening to gain empathy with others.

✔ Avoid misunderstandings.

✔ Identify negative and positive examples of listening skills.

✔ Learn to ask questions that demonstrate your listening ability.

Methodology

A workshop format that encourages participants to confront their weaknesses in listening and gain mastery over active listening techniques. Numerous exercises reinforce new habits.

Length of Program: One day.

The Center for Technical Communication (CTC), 22 East Quackenbush Avenue, Dumont, NJ 07628, phone 201-385-1220

FIGURE 5.1   Breakout session descriptive flyer.

average "working Joe" speaker who is not a celebrity or best-selling author is going to have to spend a lot of time and effort in marketing to get a shot at these engagements.

The National Speakers Association Web site, www.naspeaker.org, lists 4,000 speakers. According to an article in *Business News* (March 21, 2000), studies from the NSA indicate the average speaking fee is $3,500. If you get that for a 90-minute keynote, your rate for actual speaking time

is $2,333 an hour. That's something you can brag about to your class-
mates at your next high school reunion!

LOCAL VERSUS NATIONAL
SPEAKING OPPORTUNITIES

As a rule, national meetings of associations hire and pay professional
speakers, while local chapters use amateur speakers who speak for
free.

Speakers at the local chapters are often vendors who are giving the
speech as a way to gain visibility and generate new business leads. They
are looking for product sales or consulting income, and they view speaking as self-promotion. Since the local chapters can get these folks to speak
for free, they feel no need to pay a professional speaker to give a talk. Local chapters naturally have limited budgets, so they usually cannot afford
the fee a professional speaker wants to get.

Some local chapters do pay some speakers, on occasion. Often
they will pay an out-of-town expert a fee for a presentation, while expecting the local expert to donate his or her time in exchange for the
exposure.

Local chapters that will not pay for a lunch or after-dinner talk (the
majority) might be willing to pay you for a longer presentation, such as a
half-day seminar held in the morning or the afternoon. Although they
may barely break even on such a venture, their purpose is to generate
long-term return by recruiting as new members some of the people who
come to hear your seminar. Do not fret that your fee is too high to allow
them to make a profit just from the seminar revenues; it is the increased
membership they are looking for.

If you are targeting an industry where the custom is for vendors to
speak for free as a self-promotional tool, you will have great difficulty getting paid for a speech since there are so many volunteering to give the talk
gratis. Associations whose members represent a potentially lucrative target market for products and services usually expect that people will speak
before their group for free, in exchange for the opportunity to get leads
from the audience.

What if you aren't there to sell them anything but your ideas? You
have to make it clear to the meeting planner that the speech itself is your
product—and that speaking is your service—and that is what you are
selling. I have found that meeting planners who want informative talks
that are not sales pitches often prefer to hire paid professional speakers,

precisely because they know that the speaker, already compensated for his or her time, is not under pressure to make money by selling the audience something.

ADDITIONAL TIPS FOR SPEAKING TO THE MEETINGS MARKETPLACE

✔ Go to the next national meeting of any trade association you belong to. Listen to the keynote and attend as many breakout sessions as you can. Notice the difference in content and style. The keynote is usually more motivational, while the breakouts focus on practical, usable content or important industry issues. Which appeals to you more from a speaker's point of view?

✔ Many association meeting planners prefer speakers with experience in the industry their association caters to. Look up in the *Directory of Association Meeting Planners* or the *Encyclopedia of Associations* (ask your librarian) and make a list of the associations covering your field. Join the leading ones and participate. As a member, you have an edge in getting invited to speak. Call national headquarters, speak to the meeting planner, tell him or her you are a member, and ask what it would take for you to get an opportunity to speak at the national meeting.

✔ Once you speak successfully at an association, get a letter of recommendation from the meeting planner. Then send it to other association meeting planners in that field and related fields. The reference from your last job will help you get hired in your next job by meeting planners who cater to a similar membership.

✔ Become known within an association or, even better, an industry. Participate in committees and panels. Write articles for the association's magazine and letters to the editor of the trade journal. Be visibly active or even controversial. Lobby the editor of the industry magazine for a column in the publication; this is a quick way to instant fame within a particular group.

✔ If you feel especially comfortable and effective talking to a certain type of audience (e.g., entrepreneurs, freelancers, creative types, techies, financial types), seek out associations whose members fit that profile. Your demo video and testimonials will show the meeting planner you have a good rapport with their type of member.

SPEAKING AT MEETINGS

Thunder Lizard, a company that produces conferences on Web marketing, presents the following tips for speakers who give keynotes and breakout sessions at meetings:

✔ *Read the conference brochure copy describing your session.* Attendees expect you to deliver what's promised. Your session description is in the conference brochure. Read it before preparing your presentation, and read it again before you make the presentation. Deliver what's promised, and attendees will love you.

✔ *Give how-to.* People want to know *how* to do what you're talking about, not just why they should do it or what they should do. Tell them *how*. Golden rule: *Everybody* loves tips and tricks.

✔ *Start with an introduction, but keep the hotshots happy.* To address different audience levels, start your session with an intro to bring lower-level people up to speed, but sprinkle the intro liberally with hot tips that will keep the hotshots interested. This is especially crucial on the first morning of an event.

✔ *Address multiple levels.* Be aware that most attendees are expert in some areas, and novice-level in others. There's no such thing as generic beginner, intermediate, and advanced.

✔ *Plan the flow.* Show your second-best tip first, and your best tip last. Wow them to start with, back off to the intro, and build to the killer climax. Leave them laughing.

✔ *Match handouts to presentation.* Provide handouts that follow the course of your presentation. Attendees like to follow along. And be sure to follow your handouts. Don't make major changes to your presentation after delivering handouts. Minor changes are okay.

✔ *Include more than just bulleted talking points on your slides.* Support each of the talking points with all of the key information you're providing (including graphics, examples, forms, checklists, sample documents, resources, flowcharts, data). These detailed slides can serve as excellent handouts. Use captions and callouts liberally in handouts. People love captions and callouts.

✔ *Print black type on white.* For handouts, avoid white type on a black background. Attendees find it much easier to take notes with black type on a white background.

✔ *Don't read what's in the binder.* If you want to read a speech, don't include the printed speech in the binder. Attendees hate it when speakers read what's in the binder. The handouts should contain all the information, but not in discursive form.

✔ *Don't read your on-screen slides.* Just don't do it. People hate it.

✔ *Don't sell yourself.* If you want to promote yourself or your company or product, keep it discreet—a slide at the beginning and end, for instance. Attendees truly despise sales pitches, and you don't want them to despise you as well. The best way to win over these "customers" is wow them with well-organized and well-presented information that they need.

✔ *Repeat the question.* With questions from the audience, *repeat the question*. Not doing this is a constant complaint from attendees. It also allows you to recast a problematic question in your own terms.

✔ *Don't get sidetracked by questions.* If you get a specialized or off-topic question, don't get sidetracked. Recast the question or ask the person to see you after the session.

✔ *Check announcements with the association or conference sponsor.* Don't make announcements about materials being available without first checking with the conference staff. Attendees get angry when there aren't enough materials for everyone, or if the registration desk doesn't know what they're talking about.

✔ *Don't fight.* Don't be acrimonious. People generally like it when speakers disagree in an informative, interesting way. They *hate* it when they argue.

✔ *Be respectful of other speakers.* Again, disagreement is fine, but if all speakers show respect for all other speakers, everybody looks much better and attendees are happy.

✔ *Talk one at a time.* If you're on stage with other people, don't talk at the same time. Through the public address system it sounds like garbled gibberish.

✔ *Start and end on time.* Keep to a strict timetable. Attendees really like it when you stay on schedule.

✔ *Don't rely on questions.* You should have a structured, defined presentation ready, with enough material to fill the time (more is better). Avoid the free-form "Hey, ask any question, any time" approach. Random walks through the content usually miss the mark, and imply to attendees that you're not taking the session seriously.

It's never too late to change. It's never too late to make your life even more worthwhile. By the time you reach 50 or 60, you have a good chance of making it to 80 and even 90 years of age. For a 50-year-old, that can mean 40 more years of life. And you might as well be doing what you really want to be doing in the last 40 years of your life if you didn't have the chance to do it in the first part of your life.

—Matthew Lesko, *Free Money to Change Your Life*
(Information USA)

✔ *Carry backups.* Bring backup copies of your presentation, and, to really cover yourself, the software necessary to view your presentation (especially if it's unusual software).

✔ *Cross-reference within the event.* Attend and refer to other conference sessions in your presentations. It puts your content in context, and avoids repetition. Give the attendees in your session cross-references to other sessions.

✔ *Know your audience.* A show-of-hands survey of attendee interest/platform/experience is often taken at the opening of the event. Attend this survey or at least query the sponsor on the results so that you do not have to ask the same questions of your attendees again during your sessions.

✔ *Take off your badge before going onstage.* It reflects the spotlights and is quite distracting.

6

Market Opportunity #2: Corporate Training

WHAT IS "TRAINING"?

According to an article in *American Demographics* (February 1998, page 39), 47 percent of college-educated workers participate in skill-improvement training for their current jobs each year.

The American Society for Training and Development says that in 1995 American companies spent $55 billion on formal worker training (*Record*, June 23, 1997, page H-10, and December 22, 1997). About 60 percent of this money is spent on technical training, with the balance spent teaching soft skills—everything from leadership and assertiveness to conflict resolution, active listening, stress management, and business writing. And an article in *Money* (December 1997) notes that five million adults are taking classes to keep up or catch up with skills necessary to do their jobs.

An article in *Training & Development* (November 1997, page 53) reports that respondents to a July 1997 survey of national human resources and development executives showed that the top 10 training trends are as follows:

1. Computer skills training.
2. Teamwork training.
3. Shift from training to performance (training to achieve specific objectives or business results).

4. Decision-making and problem-solving training.

5. Rapid development and deployment of training.

6. Systems-thinking training.

7. Demonstrating training outcomes.

8. Measuring performance outcomes.

9. Shift from training to learning.

10. Making a business case for training interventions.

WHAT CAN YOU CHARGE FOR TRAINING?

For an in-house corporate training seminar, companies expect to spend around $200 to $250 per employee per day. So for a typical class with 15 employees, $3,000 to teach the class is not unreasonable. Many consultants get $1,500 a day; but some earn $4,000 a day or more. The more specialized and in-demand your program, the more you can charge.

According to an article in *Training & Development* (January 1998, page 26), the typical U.S. private sector organization with 50 or more employees spends about $504 per employee per year on training. The article says the most popular training courses offered are:

✔ New employee orientation.

✔ Management and supervisory skills.

✔ Computer literacy and applications.

✔ Job-specific technical skills.

✔ Occupational safety and compliance.

✔ Teams.

✔ Quality, competition, and business practices.

✔ Customer service.

✔ Awareness.

✔ Professional skills.

✔ Product knowledge.

✔ Executive development.

✔ Sales training.

✔ Basic skills.

Today, I would certainly add e-business, e-commerce, and other Internet-related topics to the list. Can you charge a premium for training in a hot topic like e-business? Yes, but only if you have something different or better than the competition. If a lot of trainers are offering essentially the same information as you are, and your reputation does not exceed theirs, it will be difficult to command a premium price.

OVERVIEW OF THE TRAINING MARKET

A few months ago I taught a writing seminar to a group of 25 logistics professionals employed by the U.S. Army. My fee: $6,000. The week before, I taught a shorter version of the seminar at a medical equipment company. For less than a day's work, I received $3,500 plus expenses.

The point: Speakers and consultants can earn significant fees teaching their knowledge and skills to others. In fact, with fees ranging from $1,000 to $4,000 a day, *teaching* a skill often pays better than performing the task or exercising the skill itself. Here are some steps you can take to get into the lucrative speaking, consulting, training, seminar, and workshop business.

Fortune 1000 companies are the most likely candidates to hire you to train employees. Some midsize companies also buy seminars. But as a rule, the smaller the firm, the less likely it is to have a formal training program or budget.

In-house seminars are needed in such topics as business writing, technical writing, interpersonal skills, time management, quality control, diversity in the workplace, and presentation skills. Specialty subjects, such as how to write ISO 9000 documentation or comply with OSHA requirements, are also in demand.

If you consult on a subject of interest to businesspeople—stress reduction, time management, leadership, success, selling, management, the Internet—you may find a ready market for in-house training seminars on these topics as well.

Contact corporations and offer your services as a trainer. Write to training managers. Or call vice presidents, supervisors, and department managers whose employees may need skills improvement. Prepare an outline of your course and a biography highlighting your credentials to send prospective clients who request more information. Design these materials so they can be faxed or e-mailed if there is immediate interest.

Training managers typically won't be interested in your program unless they've gotten a request from a manager in their company for a seminar on that topic. Most collect information for future reference. Send them your literature and follow up periodically by mail, fax, and phone. Don't call too often, or you will be perceived as a pest; two to four times a year is just about right.

Front-line managers and supervisors may not be thinking about a training program, but if they feel lack of skills is a problem in their organizations, your offer will interest them. Stress the benefits of skill improvement, especially any return on investment it can generate. If your program will help employees improve quality, productivity, customer service, sales, or profits, say so.

In corporate training, the client hires you on a per diem basis and sends employees to the training session you conduct. They provide the bodies, room, and refreshments. You teach the seminar and supply course materials. Class sizes typically range from 10 to 25 students, although I have had as many as 35 in a session.

Seminars, which take a half day, one day, or two days (one day seems to be the most popular length right now), are usually held in a conference room at the client's offices. Your agreement should specify the number of hours you are to train. At my office, we define a half day as two to three hours, and full day as five to six hours.

Say you don't specify, but you anticipate doing your normal six-hour day. Then you get there, and the client tells you the seminar starts at 8 A.M. and will end at 6 P.M., with an hour lunch break. Now you have to fill nine hours! You are short of material, which can create both stress and embarrassment, if not downright panic. And the client is getting more than you were paid for. Be specific about the exact hours—the start time, the finish time, and the total number of actual training hours.

In your agreement with the client, you may want to specify an additional fee above or beyond a certain number of attendees, say 20 or 25 or whatever your preferred maximum class size may be. The fee per extra attendee is up to you, but $50 to $100 per head seems reasonable. This prevents the client from trying to overstuff one session and avoid paying for a second seminar for the additional attendees. If the client has too many students in one class, the personalized attention you can give each trainee will suffer.

If the client is out of town, you'll have to travel. You don't get paid an extra fee for your travel time, but the client reimburses you for all expenses including airfare, lodging, meals, and other out-of-pocket expenses. I use the travel time to work on my program and prepare for the upcoming class. On the trip home, I tally my expenses, prepare an invoice, write the client a thank-you note, and work on consulting and writing projects I've brought with me. Be sure your agreement is clear that the client pays all expenses, including incidentals.

PUTTING YOUR PROGRAM TOGETHER

The client does not hand you a textbook or outline and say, "Teach this course." As an independent trainer, you present a program of your own design. You must supply the complete content, including handouts.

You can distribute the materials one sheet at a time or all at once in a bound workbook. The advantage of doing them one sheet at a time is that people concentrate on what is being said. If you give them a workbook, they may flip ahead out of curiosity or boredom and not pay attention to you or others in the class.

Putting together a training course is not at all difficult. Courses are organized in a similar fashion to books—except books have chapters, while courses have modules.

Therefore, if a manager at a local company asks you to present a seminar on business writing to her employees, go immediately to the bookstore and buy two or three books on the subject. You can pattern your course outline after the tables of contents in these books.

Your course should be designed as a series of modules covering various subtopics related to the major topic. The outline for my "Effective Business Writing" course, shown in Chapter 3 (Figure 3.4), lists the following eight modules:

A workbook is easier and more convenient to ship and distribute, and it has higher perceived value. Many trainers charge extra for their workbook, making it an option rather than including it in the price of the training; this increases their incremental revenue for the program. Clients will pay $10 to $25 per copy for a workbook, but not for a bunch of loose, photocopied handout sheets.

1. Overview—elements of effective business writing; tasks of the business writer (letters, memos, proposals, reports, e-mail).

2. Fundamentals of grammar—grammatical rules, punctuation, abbreviation, capitalization, spelling.

3. Principles of composition—active versus passive voice; simple versus complex language; how to write concisely; tenses; style.

4. Words and phrases—how to eliminate sexist language, redundancy, jargon, wordiness, clichés, and other ills; correct meaning and usage for commonly misused words.

5. Principles of organization—organizing business documents; executive summaries; writing the lead; use of headings and subheads.

6. Principles of communication and persuasion—how to get your reader's attention; using facts, opinions, and statistics to prove your case; determining the level and depth of information content; how to get the reader on your side; how to get the reader to take action.

7. Principles of tone—informal versus formal language; finding and using the appropriate tone; using contractions; substituting positive words for negative words.

8. Special writing concerns of corporate employees—how to write for a specific audience; tips for making a boring topic interesting; working with uncooperative collaborators; the editing, revision, and approval process.

Additional topics I've covered in my business writing seminars include editing, rewriting, research, outlining, and prewriting planning. In technical writing seminars, I have a module on illustrating writing with tables, graphs, charts, diagrams, and other visuals.

You can adjust the course to the customer's training objectives and class schedules by mixing and matching modules and topics within each module. Some modules of your seminar may have the potential to be given as complete seminars by themselves. For instance, I do a seminar on direct mail that includes such topics as copywriting, design, lists, and offers; some clients have hired me to do a full day just on direct mail copy.

As mentioned, some trainers include a set of handouts for each student as part of the cost, and pay for the photocopying out of their own pockets. Some bind their handouts in workbook format and charge the client an additional $10 to $25 for each student receiving a workbook. If you've written a book on the topic of your seminar, give the client the option of offering copies to each of the attendees. In the corporate world, the client will buy copies for the trainees and distribute the books to them; it is inappropriate to pitch your products from the platform as you might at a public lecture or association meeting.

Make your seminar entertaining as well as informative. Consider using videos, cartoons, humor, props, overheads, flip charts, games, team exercises, and other techniques to maintain attendee interest. Plan a lot of activities for the students.

Be creative in your presentation. Seminar leader Terry Smith, author of *Making Successful Presentations* (John Wiley & Sons), gets seminar attendees to participate by offering anyone who asks or answers a question a mystery prize in a sealed envelope. Terry tells the attendees that the prize may be worth one million dollars or more! Inside each envelope is a lottery ticket.

Remember, although you love your subject, some of the people in your seminar may not. In many instances, seminar attendees are forced to go to your course by their managers. A few may resent being sent. Others may resist your trying to teach them a skill they don't admire or care about. The more you can entertain as you train, the more enthusiastic your class will be, and the more they'll learn.

Keep in mind your trainees are busy adults with many things to do. Do not be disturbed if class members have to pop in and out to attend meetings, make calls, or check messages. Do not act annoyed when they do.

Show up at least an hour early. This gives you time to prepare the room and meet some of your students before class starts. Talk with students before the seminar and during breaks to get their feedback on how the day is going.

Offer some type of follow-up or support service. This can be included in the fee or sold for an extra charge. Gary Blake, a writing trainer, offers free telephone support for 30 days after the seminar. He also offers

Props are effective speaking aids. In a seminar on effective telephone selling, I had students practice conversations using toy phones. Sound effects, including dial tones and phones ringing, made the presentation fun and lively.

an editing-by-fax service where trainees fax in their work for comment and review.

Including the follow-up or support service as part of the seminar gives you an advantage when negotiating price. The addition of this extra service makes your program seem more valuable and complete, and discourages comparisons based just on fee. For instance, if the client says, "I found another company that also does seminars on Topic X and they charge $500 less than you do," you reply, "But do they offer follow-up support for trainees after the training?" That can often set you apart.

THIRTY TIPS FOR BEING MORE SUCCESSFUL IN TRAINING

Madison Gross, an experienced trainer and training manager, has had a 20+-year career dealing with hundreds of seminar leaders and instructors on behalf of universities, associations, and consulting firms. Based on this, he has come up with 30 qualities that he looks for when hiring presenters. The better you meet these requirements, the more successful you'll be at getting training and speaking assignments:

1. Connect with your audience (i.e., use eye contact and relate to all members of the audience).

2. Be prepared to come early and stay late, to meet the attendees and answer particular questions.

3. Encourage real give-and-take participation with the audience (known as the Socratic technique). Avoid lecturing at people or reading your teaching material.

4. Demonstrate practical knowledge and depth of your subject matter. Clients really don't want people who are filled with one-industry war stories.

5. Know that the best instructors have the ability to deal with all types, including the novice learner, those who possess negative attitudes, the nonparticipants, and those who are highly intelligent. Use those highly intelligent ones as mentors, and encourage them to bring up ideas and techniques to pass on to the others.

6. Remember that those who have poise and enjoy great personal presence always get better evaluations than those who don't.

7. Understand that clients look for people who are real leaders or are facilitators to teach short course programs.

8. Keep in mind that the instructor should be nonoffensive in words and examples and never condescending to members of the audience.

9. Never, ever sell your consulting services or books on the platform!

10. Demonstrate real pleasure in sharing your hard-won expertise with others.

11. Solicit questions and always answer them honestly.

12. Have a positive attitude and accept criticism constructively, especially from paying customers.

13. Be prepared and organized in arranging your material before you teach.

14. Be a bit flexible about covering sections of the course; if the discussion on a particular subject seems to be hot, try not to shut it off due to a strict time schedule.

15. Have a sense of humor and have some fun teaching.

16. Be articulate and keep working on your communication and presentation skills. Practice becoming a persuasive speaker.

17. Build up as much teaching experience as you can (including night school and association meetings) before attempting to teach adult seminars.

18. Use well-organized examples, tips, checklists, and forms. The workbook should always be kept up-to-date.

19. Don't bury the attendees in information. Check to make sure things are understood.

20. Never appear canned or rehearsed even if you've done this course hundreds of times.

21. Vary your presentation with judicious use of audiovisual techniques, and employ a variety of training methods.

22. Keep things upbeat and remain enthusiastic from beginning to end. Remember to smile often.

23. Keep focused. Don't let the discussion roll off on tangents and into side issues.

24. Have a strong opening and closing. The differences between the good and excellent ratings often lie in the first and last impressions.

25. Recognize that every class group is different from the last, and it's worth varying your presentation if you feel you didn't get off to a good start.

26. Be constantly alert to breakthroughs in your field.

27. Be profit oriented in your approach to problem solving.

28. Always explain sophisticated material in down-to-earth terms.

29. Deliver more than is promised in the promotion piece.

30. When teaching technical programs, present identifiable and understandable real-world company examples and case studies to illustrate your presentation.

SPECIAL CHALLENGES OF SPEAKING TO SMALL AND LARGE GROUPS

I have done in-house corporate training seminars with class sizes ranging from seven to 35 or more.

Once you get about 30 or so in a class, you lose some of the one-on-one interactivity that you enjoy in a more moderate-size class. For instance, in a group of 20, I like to go around the room and have each attendee give his or her name, job function, and what he or she hopes to get out of the course. If there are 60 students, though, this isn't practical, since it would take too much time.

For the larger groups, you have to focus more on lecture and less on group activities and interactions. So it becomes more of a talk and less of a workshop—a situation that may not be ideal for training, depending on your subject. You have to judge for yourself.

When a client proposes a group that is too large for optimal training—so large that, split in two, each group would accommodate your minimum acceptable class size—suggest that for best results the client hire you to do two one-day seminars. Schedule these so you can do both classes on the same trip. They should take place on two consecutive days; you don't want to waste time out of town with a down day when you are not working.

For smaller groups numbering below 10 attendees, you may also lose some of the interplay that happens in a larger group. Should you be so unlucky as to have a group of six or seven trainees, all of whom are reticent or quiet, you may not get the group dynamic you want. And to fill the dead time, you have to talk more. Again, you end up with a lecture rather than a workshop.

> Don't underestimate your worth by comparing yourself with others. It is because we are different that each of us is special.
>
> —Nancy Sim (Cited in *Dear Abby*)

If the audience is only one or two people, maybe the client should arrange for a private tutorial—the presentation of your seminar material in a one-on-one teaching session—for these trainees. Most trainers charge less for a tutorial than for a normal-size seminar class, but that again is up to you.

Chapter

7

Market Opportunity #3: Self-Sponsored Public Seminars

People go to seminars for specific how-to information covering narrowly defined topics. Seminars provide the real-life, experienced-based knowledge that these people feel they do not get from traditional academic courses.

A seminar must be extremely *practical* to be successful. General or overly broad topics are not appropriate for seminars.

Seminars are just another way to package and sell your information to the public. For example, if your expertise is in a particular field (e.g., computers, careers, child care), you can probably create an interesting one-day seminar on that topic—one that would provide people with specific information they want or need enough to pay a relatively high fee ($45 to $300) to obtain.

Many speakers are writers, and there is a synergistic effect when writers work in seminars. For example, for two years I taught a half-day seminar on "How to Promote Your Own Business." When I proposed a book on this topic to New American Library, the publisher bought it immediately. Writing the book took no research and very little time, because I had done 95 percent of the legwork in preparing for and teaching the seminar.

If the public seminar sells like gangbusters, and you can generate attendance for more sessions than you can lead personally, you can always hire someone to present your seminar. This has two drawbacks, though:

> A guest speaker who has a service or product to sell or a desire to promote himself or herself may be willing to speak at your seminar without fee in exchange for the publicity. If you must pay, I have found that I can get good speakers to present a 30- to 60-minute talk for $100. The trick is to find local people who know their subject but are not professional speakers (who charge much, much more).

First, it is difficult to find someone who can deliver your topic as authoritatively and expertly as you can. Second, the speaker's fee comes out of your pocket, lowering profits.

My advice is to give the seminar yourself. If it becomes so profitable that you want to expand into other cities, you might consider hiring people to give your program at that time. However, I have found that for a full-day seminar, I like to get a guest speaker to come in for an hour and give me a break.

WHAT MAKES FOR A GOOD PUBLIC SEMINAR TOPIC?

The topic must fit the following formula:

- ✔ It delivers how-to advice or other practical information that attendees can put to immediate use in their lives or their jobs.

- ✔ It is a topic the attendees not only need to know about but want to know about. If the topic isn't something that strongly interests people, they will not attend—even if the information is important.

- ✔ The topic can be adequately covered in the time allotted (as you will see, I recommend a one-day format for your first seminar).

- ✔ The topic must appeal to a *specific* group of people (e.g., writers, nurses, teachers, consultants, affluent people, corporate executives, entrepreneurs) who can be reached through specific media—either a mailing list or an ad in a trade journal, magazine, or newspaper.

Examples? I keep an extensive file of various seminar mailings, announcements, and invitations, and suggest you do the same (so you can

If you are creating seminars to give attendees skills to cope with their important problems, it helps to know what problems your prospects are worried about. According to an article in *Prevention*, a survey of 1,487 people found out what they worry about most.

Men

1. Cost of living.
2. Political or social problems.
3. Unexpected expenses.
4. The environment.
5. Their workload.
6. Their health.
7. Deadlines.
8. Their children.
9. Household tasks.
10. Their job.

Women

1. Cost of living.
2. Unexpected expenses.
3. Household tasks.
4. The environment.
5. Political or social problems.
6. Their health.
7. Their children.
8. Their physical fitness.
9. Their partner.
10. Their physical appearance.

Charging the lowest price for your seminar, amazingly, does not always boost response and can sometimes *decrease* response. Reason: People perceive your seminar as having less value if the price seems too low compared with the going rate.

see how successful promoters sell their seminars). Here are some topics that are successful for these sponsors:

"Motivating and Managing Salespeople."

"How to Buy Printing."

"How to Build a Profitable Consulting Practice."

"How to Earn $50,000 Profit from Your First Book."

"Systematic Software Testing."

"How to Handle Difficult People."

"The Winner's Workshop: How Sports Psychology Can Make You a Champion."

"Newsletter Writing, Editing, Design, and Production."

The best topics combine the offer of desired information with a concrete benefit (e.g., make more money, write better and faster, become a published author, retire at age 40, etc.).

Public seminars fall into two categories: those aimed at business executives and employees, and those aimed at the general public (consumers).

What are the differences?

A business seminar gives information that helps people do their jobs better, faster, or more efficiently—to save the company time or money or to improve productivity or customer service. Because the corporation is often footing the bill and the attendees are not paying out of their own pockets, you can charge more. (More about fees later in Chapter 12.)

However, because a company is paying you to train its employee, it wants information that benefits the company, not the employee specifically. Thus, "How to Be a Better Manager" would be a good topic for a one-day business seminar. "How to Get the Job You Want" would not sell to business, because no corporation is going to pay you to teach its employees to quit and get a better job in another firm!

A seminar for the general public, on the other hand, is one that individuals will attend on their own time and pay for out of their own pockets. Thus, these seminars are more price sensitive and the fee is usually a quarter to half that of a business seminar.

A consumer seminar must offer some direct benefit to the attendees that can help them improve their lives, do things they want to do, make money, look better, become financially independent, become physically fit, avoid illness, and so forth. Hence the popularity of topics like "No Money Down Real Estate Investing" or "How to Start Your Own Consulting Business."

SETTING THE REGISTRATION FEE FOR YOUR PUBLIC SEMINAR

How much money can you charge for a public seminar? For a consumer seminar, the fee range is $49 to $129, although some high-priced seminars cost more. It depends on the audience. If you are teaching doctors to invest in real estate, they may be willing to pay more (or maybe not—although they certainly can afford it!). If you are selling to a group that doesn't have much money (e.g., college students or the unemployed), the fee will have to be lower.

For my own one-day seminar, "How to Become a Published Author," I charge $99 to those who register in advance by mail and $129 for walk-in registration at the door. Feedback from participants indicates that $99 is just about right for them.

For a business seminar, the average for one day seems to be between $225 and $295 a day when aiming at middle management; $95 to $150 for secretarial and administrative staff.

Before you set the price for your own seminar, collect brochures and mailings from other seminar providers offering similar programs and see what they charge. You should charge somewhere between medium and high.

SCHEDULING YOUR PUBLIC SEMINAR

For a seminar to the general public, the best day is Saturday, because most people cannot take off from work on a weekday, and most prefer to stay home and relax with the newspaper on Sunday.

Saturday seminars are also good for you if you have a full-time job and are doing this on a moonlighting basis.

I give my "How to Become a Published Author" seminar on Saturday and, even though I am self-employed and could do it any day, prefer Saturday because it doesn't interfere with my other workload (writing and consulting with corporate clients). It brings me $1,000 to $2,500 in income on a day where I'd normally be loafing or watching TV anyway.

For business seminars, the middle of the week—Tuesday, Wednesday, and Thursday—are the best days. On Monday, most people do not have the energy and enthusiasm to get much out of a seminar. And they don't want to attend on Friday because it's so close to the weekend. Weekends, of course, are out—because employees want to go to the seminar on company time.

What months are best for public seminars? I find that there are two good seasons: March through June and September through mid-November. Summers (July, August) are bad because many people are on vacation. From mid-November through December 31st is bad because it interferes with the holiday season. January and February are not bad in themselves, but if you live in a northern climate, as I do, the threat of cancellation due to bad weather is always a possibility.

As for length, I think a one-day seminar is ideal for the beginner. Theoretically, from a money point of view, a two- or three-day seminar is better, because it can generate significantly more profit. Reason: Although the cost of marketing and promoting your seminar is the same regardless of the length of the seminar, the profit from longer seminars is greater because you can charge more: about twice the fee of a one-day session for a two-day seminar, and three times the fee for three days.

However, there are two drawbacks to the two- and three-day format. First, time is precious to many people today. As seminar expert Dr. Rob Gilbert notes: "The hard part in selling seminar attendance is not to get the attendee to part with the money—it's to get him to give up his *time*." Therefore, it's easier to get someone to commit to one day. It's much more difficult to convince people that your seminar is worth two or three days out of their busy schedules.

Second, the thought of talking for two or three days may be intimidating for the beginning speaker, and it takes a lot more time to prepare and create a two- or three-day seminar than a one-day seminar.

For these reasons, a one-day seminar is ideal. The profit potential is good, and the seminar can be prepared on relatively short notice.

A half-day seminar is generally not as profitable as a one-day seminar. Reason: Although the marketing costs are the same, people perceive that a half day is less valuable than a full day, so you cannot charge as much.

CHOOSING A FACILITY

What about location? When you do your first seminar, it's best to hold it locally, if you can. Why? Because when you're just starting out, you don't know whether your program will be a success—or a flop. So you want to keep expenses to the minimum. Holding the program locally eliminates airfare, travel, and lodging—which, in an initial effort, could mean the difference between profit and loss.

Another benefit is that you know the local market (i.e., the affluence of the community, their interests, etc.). It is also easier to find a hotel or other meeting place if the seminar is local. Finding facilities for out-of-town seminars is much more difficult. If you live in a rural area, though, you may have to go to the nearest big city to hold your seminar. Once you have experience, major cities or well-populated suburban areas near major cities are your best bet.

Choose your facility with care. There are many places that rent rooms for meetings, including:

- ✔ Colleges and universities.
- ✔ High schools.
- ✔ Junior highs.
- ✔ Libraries.
- ✔ Shopping malls.
- ✔ Hotels.
- ✔ Conference centers.
- ✔ Performing arts groups.
- ✔ Community theaters.

Some suggest that you get the cheapest place possible, and there is some logic in this. The profit margins in the seminar business are slim, and controlling expenses carefully has a big impact on the bottom line. Spending too much on the room and beverages could easily wipe out a good chunk of your profits.

Many people are not bothered by shabby facilities. But many are. It depends on your audience.

One seminar my wife attended, on how to write and sell scripts to TV and movies, was in an awful dump in New York City—in a lousy neighborhood. However, people didn't seem to mind! Perhaps, in part, it was because the seminar was so good. But another factor is that most of the people were young, struggling artists living in the Big Apple. These

> Important point: Room rates are negotiable. Hotels with unbooked rooms may quote a lower fee than those with plenty of business. It pays to shop around and get prices from at least three or four facilities before making a decision.

people are happy to meet anywhere. But if you are selling to middle-aged suburbanites (a group of which I admit being a card-carrying member), they want nice, comfortable, and safe surroundings. They will not come to a bad neighborhood.

I prefer to hold my seminars in nice suburban hotels that rent meeting rooms to seminar givers and to corporations (for meetings).

Look for a facility that is conveniently located and easy to get to by car or mass transit. I like to be able to say in my promotional literature, "Located Just Off Exit 32 on Route I-95." If the place sounds hard to get to, some people will not register because of that.

The hotel should be clean, neat, modern, and attractive. There should be dining facilities (or nearby restaurants) where attendees can eat lunch.

In a suburb, the room rate can run anywhere from $75 to $300, not including coffee and tea, which is extra.

In a big city such as New York, expect to pay $350 to $700, depending on the size of the room and the day of the week.

Always visit the hotel and see the room in person, if the seminar is local. Meet with the catering director (this is the person who handles rental of seminar rooms). Explain your plans for future seminars, and that you are looking for a facility to give all your business to. This may result in more favorable rates.

Try to get a room that will hold 50 people in classroom style. This means rows of tables with chairs behind them.

If registration is good and you get more than 50, you can switch to theater style seating: rows of chairs with no tables in front of them. A room that can hold 50 people seated classroom-style can hold 100 people seated theater-style.

Do not provide lunch. In your promotional literature say, "Lunch is on your own."

There are several reasons for this.

First, if you provide lunch the hotel will cater it, serving an unenjoyable cafeteria-quality meal at inflated prices—prices you will have to pass on to attendees in the form of a higher seminar fee, which could have a negative effect on registration. Second, most people understand the afore-mentioned point, and are happier to get a better meal at a reasonable price at a local restaurant—and they realize the benefit is a lower seminar fee. (They know there really is no such thing as a free lunch!)

If the hotel has a restaurant, inform the management of your seminar and make sure they will have enough food and waiters on hand to serve your crowd. (Although, despite promises, they will probably fall short in this regard.)

Allow at least an hour for lunch, and preferably an hour and a quarter. I know it seems like a lot—but believe me, it takes time to go to lunch, get served, pay the check, go to the bathroom, and get back. No matter how long you allow for lunch, at least half of the people will return late.

And be careful about snacks. It sounds trivial, but serving too many snacks can quickly gobble up your profits for the day!

Coffee service is where the hotel makes its money—and it's tremendously expensive. Coffee and tea service can range from $1 to $2 per person. Multiply that by 50 people, and serve two or three times a day, and it adds up.

I have coffee and tea in the morning when the attendees register, then instruct the hotel staff to leave the coffee for our midmorning break and replenish it if necessary. Then, they bring out coffee, tea, and sodas for the afternoon break. Sodas, at $1.50 each, are an expensive luxury. But I like a soda during the day.

Do not serve muffins, danish, or any other snack food. People do not need it or expect it, and it can cut substantially into your profit.

PROMOTING THE PUBLIC SEMINAR

How do you get people to register for your seminar? In most cases, the best method is direct mail: You rent a mailing list of names and send out invitations. The goal is to get them to register (and hopefully pay) in advance rather than walk in at the door.

For a seminar aimed at the general public, you want them to send a check or pay via credit card. Do not offer to bill them; half the people will not show up or honor your invoice.

For a business audience, you may have to offer a bill-me option, since many corporations operate that way. You can reduce your risk of nonpayment by asking them to sign the reply form, give you a purchase order number, or even send a purchase order with their registration. If you can get your bank to allow you to accept MasterCard and Visa, this can increase response 10 to 20 percent.

Getting the right mailing list is the most essential element of successful seminar marketing—and the most difficult. Ideally, you want a list of people who are proven seminar attendees (or who at least buy information by mail) and have a proven interest in your subject matter—and who are geographically located near where you plan to give the seminar.

Example: For my seminar, "How to Become a Published Author," I mail to the active subscribers list of *Writer's Digest* magazine. I mail to New Jersey subscribers if the seminar is in New Jersey; Manhattan subscribers if the location is in New York City.

Lists are generally rented from firms called "list brokers." Some of these are listed in Appendix E under "Mailing Lists."

Now let's talk about creating your mailing piece. As a rule of thumb, for public seminars "self-mailers"—mailers without envelopes—generally work better than regular "packages" (mailings sent in a #10 outer envelope with a sales letter, flyer, order card, and business reply envelope). But, you might try both formats to see which works best for you.

The best way to learn how to create seminar mailings is to study those of successful seminar companies. Try to get on the mailing lists of seminar providers that have been proven successful. One you can write to for more information on its seminars and to be put on its list is:

Performance Seminar Group
204 Strawberry Hill Avenue
Norwalk, CT 06851

The basic format for selling business seminars is an 11-by-17-inch sheet of paper folded once to form four pages. For lower-priced consumer seminars, you might be able to get away with an $8^1/_2$-by-11-inch or $8^1/_2$-by-14-inch format.

If you are a good writer and understand marketing, and you think you can create a successful direct-mail piece—go to it. You may want to hire a professional copywriter or consultant to write or critique your work. This is a good idea and can probably save you a lot of money, but for the beginner it's expensive. (Also, a lot of the top professionals in the field don't like to work with beginners.)

Your seminar mailing should contain the following elements:

1. The title of the program.
2. A description of the program.

3. The benefits the reader will get if he or she registers for the program.

4. A list of bulleted items describing the specific things the reader will learn in the seminar. The more complete the list is, the better.

5. Testimonials from others who have taken the seminar (if available).

6. Instructor's biography and qualifications to lead the seminar.

7. Date and hours of the seminar.

8. Name of hotel, address, and location.

9. Fee.

10. Registration coupon and instructions on how to register.

11. Cancellation policy.

12. Food arrangements (lunch provided? coffee? tea?).

13. Phone number to call in case the reader has questions.

14. Incentive for early registration, if any (can be a discount, free gift, or limited seating).

What kind of results can you expect from your mailing? Seminar mailings will produce anywhere from 0.25 percent to 3 percent response, with 0.5 percent to 1 percent being a typical figure. If you mail 5,000 pieces and get 0.75 percent response, your registration will be 38 people. At $99 per person, your revenue is $3,712.50. If the mailing cost you $2,200, your gross profit is $1,512.50. If the room rental is $100 and coffee and tea run $200, your net profit is $1,212.50.

On the other hand, if it was a business seminar at $275 a head, the same results would yield a profit of $7,950. Obviously, business seminars, with their higher registration fees, offer greater profit potential. However, you have to balance this with whether you desire to present to business-people or to the public at large. Maybe you can do both.

To calculate the profit, subtract your costs (direct-mail expenses plus hotel charges) from your revenues (seminar registration fees collected).

If you are making $1,000 or more for the day, you are doing pretty well. And $2,000 or more per day is super. To increase profits, sell your books, tapes, and other learning materials at the back of the room before registration and during the breaks. This can easily double your gross. Offer attendees a discount of 10 percent on a package of your materials if they place the order that day.

If you only break even on your first seminar, don't be disappointed. If you can fine-tune the program by improving your mailing package, finding a better mailing list, or cutting costs, you can turn a marginal program into a winner.

However, if you lost a lot of your money, you have to retrench and rethink your idea. Maybe another topic, aimed at a different audience, would do better.

How far in advance of the seminar should you mail? I mail my seminar invitations third-class about eight to nine weeks in advance of the seminar date. Based on a thorough study of the seminar mailings that cross my desk, I would say that most arrive in my mailbox four to eight weeks in advance of the date.

Chapter

Market Opportunity #4: Colleges and Public Seminar Companies

lthough the least lucrative of speaking markets, colleges and adult education programs are by far the easiest to break into. Public seminar company opportunities, although also low-paying, are difficult to break into, but offer a lot of prestige and help build credentials. This chapter shows how to get into these markets.

PUBLIC SEMINAR COMPANIES

An alternative to running the seminar yourself is to find a sponsor. This might be a public seminar company, adult education center, community

Many speakers break in by giving free talks. Then when they build experience and demand, they go to work in the high-paying corporate and association markets. The low-pay college and public seminar companies give you an intermediate transition step, where you can get paid yet not have the pressure of a high-fee keynote performance.

college, continuing education program, YMCA, or local university—anyplace that gives courses aimed at adults instead of regular students.

Send them a description of your program. If interested, they will contact you. Then it is up to you to negotiate your fee.

You might ask for a flat fee or per diem—anywhere from $300 to $1,000 per day. Or, you might be paid a percentage of the registration fees—anywhere from 20 to 50 percent.

There is no standard. It is really up to you. However, your goal should be to make $500 to $1,000 per day for your efforts.

Appendix D lists the biggest public seminar companies and organizations. They include the American Management Association (AMA), Fred Pryor (Pryor Resources, Inc.), and CareerTrack.

These firms regularly hire speakers both to give topics they already have as well as to create new programs. If they want you to teach a topic they already offer, they will provide a prewritten course including a teacher's guide and handouts, and expect you to give their course, not yours.

The per diem pay is low, ranging from $200 to $400. A former executive at the American Management Association told me, "We get some top speakers at these rates because it's great exposure for them. Although they are not allowed to promote themselves outright at the class, they often get hired for nice fees by attendees to give private in-house classes at the attendees' companies."

I have spoken with a couple of the big public seminar organizations and found, to my surprise, that even for an experienced speaker or established subject matter expert, they are pretty inflexible about fees. They seem not willing to pay a premium for a more qualified presenter, and prefer to hire someone who is competent, not necessarily great, but who will work within their fee structure.

The pay to develop a new course for these organizations is better—several thousand dollars—but still not great compensation for the work involved. An ancillary benefit is that some of these companies, most notably CareerTrack, will produce and market a video of you talking about your topic if they like you as a speaker. This adds to your prestige and helps attract new customers.

Since these firms are flooded with applications from candidates who want to present for them, your odds of becoming their next presenter for an established topic like business writing or stress management are slim. A better strategy is to obtain and study their course catalogs. Look for new topics or niches within existing categories, then offer to create and give a program to fill that need. The AMA wasn't interested in having me do a generic selling course, but their interest was piqued when I suggested a specialized program on the selling of services (the topic of one of my books) as opposed to products.

Another way to break into the public seminar market (aside from self-sponsoring your own seminars as discussed in Chapter 7) is to offer to do seminars for specialized associations or for seminar and conference companies catering to specialized markets.

The competition is less fierce than with the big-name CareerTracks and AMAs. The association executives feel obligated to bring education to their members and are more open to new ideas, especially innovative programs that target their niche needs.

For instance, my friend Steve Manning got the ICLE (Institute of Continuing Law Education) to sponsor a seminar on how to write a book. Why would a seminar sponsor catering to lawyers sponsor such a topic? The idea was that writing a book is a good way to promote your law practice. (Look at Alan Dershowitz and Gerry Spence, to name two lawyers whose fame is partly owed to being authors.) If you can show how your topic benefits a particular audience, seminar sponsors that target those audiences may hire you.

In many cities, you will find catalogs of courses distributed on street corners or mailed to residents. These may be from the local YMCA, a town adult education program, or a private seminar company such as the Learning Annex in New York, San Francisco, and Toronto. Contact the program director and see whether the sponsor might be interested in having you do a class on your topic.

The pay again is extremely modest, but it's good exposure and good practice. For a year or so, I gave monthly seminars in two topics—how to write a book and get it published and how to make a six-figure income as a freelance writer—for the Learning Annex in New York.

It was fun and there were several benefits. I was able to take my course handouts for how to write a book, turn them into a book on that subject, and sell it to a small publishing house. So even though I no longer give the seminars, I now get royalty payments on the book sales. I also recorded the seminar and sold it as a six-cassette audio album for $50.

As in every area of speaking, celebrities get paid the most for speaking for public seminar companies. Anthony Robbins recently paid Donald Trump $100,000 for a 35-minute talk at one of his motivational seminars.

HOW TO GET COLLEGE AND
ADULT EDUCATION BOOKINGS

Another large market is the adult and continuing education market, which focuses on teaching adults and is often sponsored by a local college or university. If your town or city has continuing education programs, you no doubt have seen their mailings and catalogs. If not, you can see whether there are such programs near you by contacting the American Association for Adult and Continuing Education and the National University Continuing Education Association, both listed in Appendix D.

As I warned at the beginning of this chapter, the chapter deals with low-paying venues, and continuing education is no exception. However, there is no better education for the new speaker than to teach adults at the continuing education college level. You learn how to teach and deal with adult learners, as the grown-up students are referred to in the continuing education world. And you learn how to prepare, organize, and give a full-length modular course. Best of all, you are being paid while you are learning, and you have an eager group of students upon which you can practice. Their feedback tells you what works in the classroom and what needs to be fixed.

Adult and continuing education programs are constantly in need of teachers. It is usually not difficult to get hired. The reason: Turnover is high. People agree to teach for the prestige, because it sounds fun, or for other reasons. When they realize how much work it is, they don't come back next semester. Or if they return for the next semester, most get burned-out within a couple of years and quit.

Also, the world is changing rapidly, so there is always a need for new courses to address these new topics. If you can't get invited to teach one of the existing courses, propose a new one. If it fills a need or a gap in the course offerings, the institution will be glad to take it.

When my first book was published—a how-to book on technical writing—my coauthor Gary Blake and I asked New York University if it would be interested in having us teach an adult education course in its School of Continuing Education. This we did for several years until we got tired of it.

Then I wanted to teach copywriting, but NYU already has a copy-writing course. I suggested a course on my specialty, business-to-business copywriting, which was agreed to and which I taught for several more years.

Eventually I took the material from the copywriting course and turned it into a book. In the course, students completed assignments and brought in samples of copy they were producing in their companies; I used these (with their permission) both in my book as well as in copywriting seminars I did for corporate clients. In fact, I turned both my NYU courses—technical writing and copywriting—into seminars that I gave to corporate clients at a rate of $3,500 a day. You can see the course outlines posted on my Web site at www.bly.com.

TWELVE TIPS FOR GETTING HIRED BY PUBLIC SEMINAR COMPANIES AND CONTINUING EDUCATION PROGRAMS

1. Prepare a one-page fact sheet on each program you want to offer.

2. Contact the dean of the continuing education program or the president or program director of the public seminar company. Call first to get the person's name, so when you write you can address correspondence to the correct individual directly.

3. Ask if an instructor is needed for an existing course that you are qualified to teach. Give your qualifications and send your bio or resume.

4. Review the course catalog and suggest new courses that complement existing programs. For instance, if you speak on e-business and the organization has a course on building your Web site, suggest a complementary course on enabling your Web site for e-commerce.

5. If the organization is not interested in the class you propose, ask what it is looking for. If a course it wants to do sounds interesting to you, suggest that you can create and teach the program for the sponsor.

6. Be willing to accept the standard fees, terms, and conditions. Arguing or insisting on compensation above the usual pay scale will make the sponsor disinclined to work with you. Remember you are taking this gig not to get rich, but to get established.

7. Do not be a prima donna. Follow the sponsor's procedures. Collect registration cards. Grade homework assignments. Hand out and collect any forms the sponsor wants the student to complete. Provide materials and information requested—neatly, accurately, and promptly. Treat the sponsor like a client. Don't be difficult or argumentative.

Do you have an idea for a new speech or seminar? Then act on it now. Why? If you don't, someone else will. Says speaker Joe Vitale, "The universe seems to supply the same idea to more than one person at a time, in a way to guarantee that the idea gets born. If you don't act on that idea, somebody will act on it. It's okay if they do, of course. But in marketing, the first to bring out the idea is usually the first to own the brand in the public's mind for that idea. In short, act now."

8. If you are hired to teach a course, do whatever you can to help the sponsor get attendees to register for your program. Promote the course on your Web site and link to the sponsor's for online registration. Do a special mailing of the course promotion to your mailing list.

9. Supply the sponsor with an updated bio. Any new achievements (e.g., a new book you have written on your topic) may help draw students to your class.

10. Never say anything bad about the sponsor in front of your class (e.g., "We would have had textbooks but the college goofed on ordering.").

11. Cross-promote in your class other classes the sponsor offers if appropriate (e.g., "That topic is covered in Advanced Direct Marketing Methods 102.").

12. Never badmouth another instructor or criticize his or her course content. If your viewpoint is different, just explain so, and say you are teaching the methods that have worked best for you. Don't say the other instructor is wrong or his or her information incorrect.

Chapter

Chapter

Marketing Yourself to Meeting Planners

For speakers who want to do keynote and breakout sessions at major association and corporate meetings, your target is the meeting planner.

A meeting planner is responsible for planning and coordinating a meeting, a complex task that involves many details, from choosing a hotel and catering meals to registering attendees and having conference programs printed.

For large organizations and events, these people may be full-time meeting planners. Meeting planning is their job and they are focused on making every meeting a success. The quality of the meetings is how they are evaluated on their performance reviews at work.

For smaller organizations or events, or even with some large ones, the person running the event may be a part-time meeting planner. He or she has another job responsibility, and planning the meeting is *in addition to* this main responsibility; it is not his or her full-time or even primary job.

A sales manager, for example, may plan a company's annual sales meeting, or may delegate the planning and coordination of the meeting to someone on the staff, perhaps a regional sales manager or inside salesperson. That salesperson may in turn plan the meeting or hire a freelance meeting planner.

The point is that meeting planners are busy people, whether meeting planning is an additional responsibility or a full-time job. In my view the number one mistake speakers make in marketing their services to meeting planners is not recognizing how busy the planners are and not respecting their time.

To you, especially if you are just breaking into the speaking business, getting hired to do the speech is the most important thing in your world. To the meeting planner, it's just one item on a long to-do list, and not even at the top of the list, at that.

Fern Dickey, a former meeting planner with the National Association of Printers and Lithographers (NAPL), a trade association for printers, shares her experience and advice on reaching meeting planners like her:

> I got an unbelievable amount of sales calls—mostly from speakers and hotel salespeople. There was no way to handle the volume. At first, I told speakers to send me information for our files—but there was no time for me or my staff to sort through all the material. We had even gotten together with another department and were going to hire a part-time person to make a spreadsheet for us and get all the speaker stuff in order. We were going to have a process for speakers to follow if they wanted to be considered (i.e., submitting certain data, giving us references, writing a letter explaining how they could help our members).
>
> We never did hire the part-time person or put together the process, because I left. I think the process would have been a good idea because it would have weeded out the less serious contenders.
>
> I spoke to potential speakers if they seemed to know about the industry or about the association. If I were a speaker I would call and ask for a packet of information about the association and its conferences and seminars. That way, when I called back I could say, "Gee, I think I could fit nicely as a breakout speaker at your Sheetfed Pressroom Conference. I'm an expert at color proofing."
>
> Very few speakers did such homework. Many seemed to go through association or meeting planner directories and make cold calls. There was no reason that I should hire them and there was no need on my end. Then they would keep calling back to see if there was a need, and there never was!
>
> I, of course, spoke to speakers who were referred by members or board members. These people probably had a better shot than most of speaking with me and getting my attention.

There were many speakers who I had to specifically ask *not* to call me again because they followed up so often and so needlessly—and some of them continued to call even after I asked them not to. I would never work with someone who did that. I also didn't like it if speakers went over my head, and called the vice president or president to try to get their attention. I can understand them pushing hard to get their foot in the door, but it doesn't make for a comfortable working relationship with the meeting planner. I think sending a newsletter or an e-mail is a lot less in-your-face and doesn't interrupt your time like a phone call.

It was hard for me to talk with speakers who had a big spiel or who were very "salesy." Lots of times their demeanor and manner of speaking took away from the call. Motivational and sales speakers were the worst offenders. In fact, lots of times they pretended they knew me. I hated that.

I liked people who were down-to-earth, knew about my association, and had a specific topic in mind to propose to me. I liked people who sent stuff first, then followed up with a call. I liked people who sent tapes (audio or video), because that's one of the best ways to judge potential speakers for a meeting.

I think meeting planners need to have a screening process in place (which we didn't), and I think speakers have an obligation to make sure they know who they're calling and if they really can fill a need for the specific audience.

WHERE TO FIND MEETING PLANNERS

Two good reference sources are the *Directory of Association Meeting Planners & Conference/Convention Directors* and the *Directory of Corporate Meeting Planners*. Updated annually, the directories list thousands of association and corporate meeting professionals. Listings indicate professional speaker usage as well as size and number of meetings, destinations, lengths, and schedules.

The *Encyclopedia of Associations* lists associations by industry or specialty (pharmaceutical manufacturers, lawyers, photographers, wholesalers) and gives the names of the key executives in charge. Its coverage is fairly comprehensive. Another source of association executive names, though not as complete, is the membership roster of the American Society of Association Executives.

Many meeting planners subscribe to *Successful Meetings* magazine and are members of Meeting Planners International (MPI). All of these resources are listed in Appendixes A and D.

FOURTEEN TIPS FOR MARKETING YOUR SPEAKING SERVICES TO CORPORATE AND ASSOCIATION MEETING PLANNERS

1. Understand the industry the association covers and the needs of its members. With practically every organization having a Web site, there is no excuse for a speaker not to be familiar with the association's goals and mission when calling to sell a seminar.

2. If you can't be bothered to research an association before you target it as a prospective speaking client, why should the meeting planner waste his or her time educating you about their needs? Think about it.

3. On cold calls, always confirm that you are speaking to the person responsible for hiring speakers for meetings. If not, ask for the name of that person. When you call that person, say "Joan Smith [or whoever you spoke to first] gave me your name." It's true, and it will get the person to listen to you for at least a few seconds.

4. When speaking to the person who hires speakers, ask whether there is an upcoming meeting for which speakers will be hired. If speakers are already booked for the entire meeting, ask when the next meeting is for which speakers will be needed, and when you should call back to discuss the needs for that program.

5. A meeting planner who is busy preparing for this week's meeting and already has speakers booked has no time to talk to speakers about the next meeting. Until the current meeting is over, that's in the future. If the meeting planner is busy with an upcoming meeting, call a week or two after that. This is enough time for things to settle down, and the meeting planner will finally be able to focus on you as a speaker for a future need.

6. Get programs for organizations' current meetings, if they will share them with you. Study the courses and suggest a session— one in which you have expertise—that might fill a gap in a cur-

rent program. A global conference on e-business, for instance, might be interested in your specialized knowledge of how to take orders in foreign currency on the Internet.

7. Ask meeting planners what topics they need that they have not been able to find speakers for. If you do not cover these topics, recommend colleagues who do, or even go out of your way to find speakers to recommend to the planners. They will be thankful that you helped them fill a need, and amazed that you took the time even though you didn't profit from it. Your star will rise in their eyes, and they will consider finding a slot for you a priority when a need for your subject arises.

8. When you see an article relating to the meeting planner's business or industry, clip and send it to the planner to keep in touch and show you are thinking of him or her. Attach a handwritten Post-It note that says, "FYI—thought this might interest you," and sign your name. Even better, write the note on your business card and attach it to the clipping with a paper clip.

9. Do not pester meeting planners by calling too frequently. If frequent calling causes the prospects to cringe when they hear it's you calling, that diminishes your chances of ever getting hired. It does not improve them.

10. When meeting planners express interest, do not get excited. It just means they're considering you as one of their speakers for one of their events. No commitment has been made. They have not promised anything and don't owe you anything. Don't act as if they do, or they'll cross you off their lists.

11. Do not use hard-sell tactics in an attempt to close sales and get meeting planners to book you before they are ready. They won't. There are dozens of speakers they can choose from, and they'll make their choices when they are ready to do so. If you attempt to pressure them into hiring you today, it may backfire and get you eliminated from the running. Meeting planners have lots to juggle, and they move according to their schedules, not yours.

12. If you want to contact the meeting planner but feel another phone call would be pestering, use an alternative means. E-mail in particular is ideal for keeping in touch without having to force busy people to have a conversation with you. E-mail is also the most convenient medium for them to reply.

13. If you notice a trend, like e-business or ISO certification, and get the bright idea to capitalize on it by teaching a seminar, you are

We can change. We can be different. We can defy our personal history. Our past is only a memory carried into a present moment. In the present moment, we can change it all. We do so by changing our point of view . . . by changing our beliefs.

—Barry Neil Kaufman, Founder, The Option Institute

already too late. The people who own the niche the trend covers are the ones who were doing it as a subject before it became popular.

14. However, a strategy that does work is to take a topic you do, customize it for a particular industry, and then go after meeting planners who work in that industry. Meeting planners prefer speakers who seem to be specialists or at least have knowledge or experience in their industries over generalists.

Chapter

Marketing Yourself to Training Directors and Human Resources Departments

My main market for speaking is corporate training. A lot of speakers do corporate training, but most I meet prefer to target association and corporate meetings, rather than in-house corporate training classes. Why is this so?

Speakers like meetings—keynotes in particular—because the pay is higher and the sessions shorter. They can go in, speak for an hour in front of a large group that applauds at the end, get $3,000, and leave.

Corporate training, by comparison, is more intensive and in-depth. The talks last a day, not an hour. Your audience is only one or two dozen people, not hundreds.

But I prefer corporate training because, in my opinion, you can deliver more benefit to your audience and make more of a difference in their businesses, their jobs, and their lives. In a one-hour keynote, you may motivate and even fascinate, but how much real learning takes place? How much do listeners get they can take back to the office and actually implement the next day?

In a one- or two-day in-house class of limited size, you do more than entertain; you actually teach and transfer knowledge and skills from yourself to the audience. Training is closer in format and approach to a college

> The purchase of training is sometimes not straightforward. Some line managers will go through their training departments for every training need. Others will bypass the training department (and have the authority to do so) and hire trainers directly. If there is a conflict between training and line management, do not get involved. Work for whoever can hire you and pay your bill. Your only responsibility is to this client.

course than it is to a speech, except obviously the time frame is compressed and the content is practical, not theoretical.

Reaching the corporate market is a little bit tricky because it is not always certain who hires you. However, there are generally two different groups of training buyers within a large corporation.

The first are training professionals: In many large corporations seminar leaders are hired either by a training manager who works under human resources (HR) or, if the company is not large enough to have a training manager, by the HR director or another HR manager. These folks are training *buyers*, not end users. They are not buying your program for themselves. Instead, like a purchasing agent, they are buying your services for someone else in their corporation: an executive who wants to train his or her team to improve their skills.

The second market for training is line managers, typically at the vice president or department head level, in charge of departments or functional areas. These are the *end users* of training: the managers who will send their staff members through your program. The sales manager, for instance, might want someone to train the sales team in closing skills. A vice president of engineering or manufacturing might need a consultant to teach a seminar to the staff on new changes in ISO quality standards.

CHOOSING YOUR TARGET

Which audience—the training department or the functional managers—is better? You can market successfully to either or both, and I have. Having done that, however, I will go out on a limb and say that it's usually better to target the functional managers directly.

A few years ago, I did a little telemarketing test for my small training

The training professional buys only if training has been identified as something to do. The line manager can be persuaded to buy training even if he or she has never thought about it, if you can identify a business problem that your training program can solve. Therefore, you have a better chance of getting more people interested when contacting end users than when contacting training professionals who are merely purchasers.

firm to generate prospects with an interest in having us do an in-house seminar in effective technical writing.

The training directors were interested, but their main interest was in getting our literature to put in their files for future reference. If they did not have a request on the table that day from a manager who wanted a technical writing seminar, there was nothing we could say to create that need or make it more urgent for them. Clearly they functioned largely as purchasing professionals filling requests from their "clients"—the managers throughout their organizations whom they serve.

Vice presidents and department managers were different. They may not have ever thought about doing a technical writing seminar. But we asked them, "Do your engineers write as clearly as you want them to? Do they struggle with their writing, and take too much of their time to write and your time to edit their work?" That got the attention of many of the managers we spoke with. It started conversations about their writing problems, and resulted in several engagements for us.

TIPS FOR MARKETING AND SELLING TO THE CORPORATE TRAINING/HR PROFESSIONAL

1. Understand the training department's buying cycle and process. If they do not have a need from someone in the company for a seminar on your topic, you cannot create the need for them. The training department buys to fill requests, not to solve business problems.

2. Should you go over training's head directly to the end users? Don't make it confrontational. Market to both the training departments *and* the end users. Training directors are just as happy to have end users come to them with both a request for

a program as well as the name of a trainer to handle it. The training department has no proprietary interest in searching for and finding a speaker; if the client wants you, the training department would just as soon hire you and make everyone happy. In fact, this is advantageous for the training professional: It's less work than having to go out and search for a trainer. And if the program is not well received, the training department is freed of blame because the user, not training, selected you.

3. Speak their lingo. The first thing a training professional will ask you about your program is, "What are your learning objectives?" This is fancy language for what the course covers and what the students will be able to do after they take the program.

4. The premier society for training professionals, the American Society for Training and Development (ASTD), is listed in Appendix D. If you intend to do a lot of work in the corporate training market, membership is very worthwhile. The members are mostly training managers, so the membership directory makes for a good prospecting list.

5. Get involved with your local ASTD chapter. See if you can get on the program to speak on your topic at one of the meetings.

6. Since training managers are often collecting information on consultants for future rather than immediate needs, they are receptive to a mailing that offers a package of information on you and your program. Include a reply card they can drop in the mail to request this information without calling you.

7. If you specialize in a narrow topic and get requests for other topics you don't handle, make a list of speakers who do handle those topics you can refer prospects and clients to. Whenever a training manager has a need you can't fill, refer him or her to the appropriate person. If they see you as a resource, they'll be more likely to favor you with their business when requests for your topic arrive on their desks.

8. Training managers are sometimes treated as low on the corporate totem pole by their own organizations, but you should treat them as the professionals that they are. Ask the training manager when you are hired about the idiosyncrasies of the organization and attendees as they relate to the seminar you are giving. That inside view will help you give a better session, and the manager will appreciate the fact that you asked.

9. Ask if there are controversial topics you should avoid. My pre-program questionnaire has a space for the training manager to indicate these topics to me. Do not spend time on subjects the training manager has asked you to avoid, even if you feel they are important.

10. Do not fight or argue with trainees. If a particular attendee is giving you a problem, quietly notify the training director during a break.

TEN TIPS FOR SELLING DIRECTLY TO END USERS OF TRAINING

1. Corporate managers do not want to buy "training"; they want to solve business problems. If you can prove that your seminar can help solve that problem, the manager will hire you to teach a class for employees.

2. Corporate managers hate the jargon training professionals use. Do not use educational lingo; use down-to-earth language. Avoid talking about "learning objectives." Tell the prospect: If you hire me to do this seminar, you can expect this result.

3. Do research to document the importance of solving the problem your seminar addresses. The prospect has many difficulties to solve, and assigns priority based on urgency and importance to the organization of getting results in that particular area. When I offered my seminar on "Effective Technical Writing" to the pharmaceutical industry, I did not say that good technical writing makes letters easier to read; I pointed out that FDA submissions rejected by the Food and Drug Administration because of unclear writing delayed time to market, potentially costing the company millions of dollars.

4. The more you can tie in your program to the company's bottom line, the easier it will be to convince managers to hire you. That's why sales training is an easier sell than, say, business writing. A 10 percent increase in sales ability can mean an extra one million dollars in revenue for a company with $10 million annual sales. It is more difficult to demonstrate the return on training investment for a business writing seminar that teaches managers how to avoid grammar mistakes.

5. When you ask past clients to send testimonials, ask them to include the business results your program helped their teams achieve: improved productivity, reduced operating costs, increased sales. Ask them to quantify with dollar amounts and percentages, if they are willing. It's very powerful to say, "My program saved Company X $600,000 a year in manufacturing costs."

6. Training managers are bombarded by marketing efforts from every speaker on every topic; line managers are not as heavily targeted. Therefore, if you can convince line managers that your topic is beneficial, they are likely to hire you rather than audition a lot of competing speakers—largely because they don't know any.

7. Sell the results your seminar can help the manager achieve, but do not overpromise. Don't say it's guaranteed to increase efficiency 15 percent if you cannot guarantee that. Do say that it has helped others increase efficiency 15 to 20 percent or more, if you have the testimonials and client references to back it up. Put your best foot forward, but do not make promises you can't keep.

8. Include some type of follow-up or support service the attendees can access for a limited time after the seminar day. This time period could range from a month to a year. The support might be a Web site, recorded telephone hot line, or ability to ask you questions via e-mail. Then stress to buyers the value of this support: how you stick with the attendees rather than just give the seminar and leave, as others do.

9. Assess the needs and skill levels of each attendee the client is sending. Do this prior to the seminar date. Let the client know you do this without charge (it's included in your total fee, as is the support) to ensure optimum training results. The assessment form I use for my business and technical writing seminars is shown in Appendix F. Send the client copies of your needs as-

If you do not know what you want out of life, then you are a lost individual from the get-go.

—Roy Jones Jr., Professional Boxer
(Cited in *Energy* Magazine)

sessment form for attendees to complete and return prior to your session date.

10. In conversation, ask the manager, "If there was one thing you wanted this seminar to do for you, what would it be?" Then make sure that concern, if nothing else, is totally addressed in the classroom.

11

Promoting Yourself on the Internet

Every speaker should have a Web site focusing on his or her area of expertise. Next to a published book, nothing establishes you as an authority more than having your own dedicated Web site on a topic.

Conversely, *not* having a Web site is a detriment to your self-marketing. Potential clients who get interested in you want to learn about you fast. If they can't access your materials online, they may choose someone else whose information is readily available on the Web. Also, speakers are supposed to be cutting edge, and not having a Web site definitely marks you as low-tech.

The ideal Web site for a speaker is a combination of information about you, your topic, and your programs. Perhaps you, like me, are not a full-time speaker but speak *in addition* to being a practitioner in your field (e.g., I am a full-time direct marketing writer and consultant who also speaks on direct marketing to associations and at in-house corporate training seminars). If this is the case, be sure to have a separate area of your site, accessible from your home page, that focuses specifically on your seminars.

WEB SITES MUST MEET MARKETING OBJECTIVES . . . AND MANY DON'T

Since putting up my Web site www.bly.com in April 1998, I've received a ton of unsolicited e-mails, faxes, and phone calls—from casual Internet

Do not overdesign your Web site. The more graphics you put into it, the slower the pages download to the viewer. According to Zona Research, Web pages take anywhere from 3 to 11 seconds to download, depending on the user's modem and Internet connection. The average viewer will "bail out"—click off the site onto another—if a page takes more than 8 seconds to download. Zona estimates these bail-outs cost e-businesses $4.35 billion annually in revenue lost from people who bail out of sites. Speed makes the difference; one site decreased its bail-out rate from 30 percent to 8 percent just by reducing its download time by 1 second per page. One survey found that 84 percent of Web sites examined downloaded too slowly.

—*Business News*, August 23, 1999

surfers as well as Web professionals—with all sorts of advice on how to make my Web site better.

Unfortunately, more than 90 percent of their suggestions are almost totally off the mark and would be a complete waste of my time and money.

Why is this the case? It's not that site visitors don't have valid opinions on graphics or content, or that Web professionals don't have good ideas. They do.

The problem is, the advice is given with no thought as to the business objective of my site and whether the enhancement would further this goal.

For example, a Web consultant called and said: "You are not getting nearly as much traffic as you should. I can help you get much more." He would advise me, he promised, on how to help my Web site get more hits than the New York Yankees. I politely explained I had absolutely no desire to increase hits to my Web site, and was not interested in what he was selling.

Frankly, he was baffled. Maybe you are, too. "Who doesn't want more hits on their Web site?" you might be thinking. The answer: plenty of folks.

Before you can meaningfully enhance a Web site, you need to understand the business of the person or company sponsoring that site as well as the business objectives they want the site to achieve.

In the case of www.bly.com, I'm a freelance copywriter, consultant, and speaker specializing in direct marketing. I serve a higher-end clientele—major direct marketers, Fortune 500 companies, and substantial technology firms—and charge accordingly.

This makes me different from many entrepreneurs who have Web sites—in two important ways.

First, 99.99 percent of people cruising the Internet are simply *not my prospects.* I'm highly selective, and don't work with small firms, start-ups, mom-and-pop operations, home-based businesses, and wanna-be entrepreneurs—precisely the mass market that's cruising the Internet looking for free marketing information and advice.

(It will be the same with you. Design your Web site mainly for your primary audience: people who can hire you to speak. If casual Web surfers visit the site and read your material, that's nice, but what does it really buy you?)

Second, with more business than we can handle, our office (I have two assistants) can't waste time responding to low-level leads. Handling inquiries from casual Internet surfers takes time and effort, and we need to devote those limited resources to the needs of our many ongoing clients.

(Again, it will be the same with you. Responding to and following up inquiries takes your most precious commodity: time. Do not invite inquiries from anyone who is not a prospect with the authority, desire, and budget to hire you to speak. Doing otherwise is a pure waste of time.)

Then why do I have a Web site? That's the key relevant question, and it's one almost no one who seeks to advise me asks.

My Web site exists primarily for instant inquiry fulfillment to qualified prospects—both for consulting and for speaking. What does that mean? Before the Internet, when a serious prospect called, we'd send an information package describing my services. That meant a lot of Priority Mail and overnight courier bills. And even with overnight shipping, prospects often waited up to 24 hours to get their hands on the material.

Having a Web site eliminates that cost and wait. When a prospect wants a package, we can send it, but we first ask, "Do you have access to the Web?" If they do, we send them to www.bly.com, where they can instantly get all the information they need to make a decision about using my services.

What should that information be? In his book *Roger C. Parker's*

Guide to Web Content and Design (MIS Press), my friend Roger Parker says content should consist of two components:

1. Information your prospects need to know in order to buy from you.
2. Information you know that will convince prospects to buy from you.

My Web site covers both these areas. The "need to know" stuff includes:

✔ An overview of my services (our home page).
✔ An online portfolio of my copywriting samples.
✔ Pages on each major service (copywriting, consulting, copy critiquing, seminars).
✔ My credentials (on an "About Bob Bly" page).
✔ Client testimonials and list.

The stuff that helps convince prospects that I'm the person they should hire to write their copy includes:

✔ Descriptions of the business books I've written.
✔ Samples of how-to articles I've written on marketing.
✔ A list of recommended vendors that shows I have the connections to help potential clients get whatever they need done.

As you see, my Web site is totally oriented toward the needs of my potential clients, and hardly at all to the casual Web surfer. But does this mean I don't want *you* to visit www.bly.com? Not at all.

On the contrary: I invite you to stop by. You may enjoy reading and downloading the free articles I've posted (click on How-to Articles). And I'd be pleased and happy if you clicked on Publications and bought any of my books (though you would not be buying them directly from me—our publication page links to amazon.com, from which we get a 15 percent commission on every book sold through our site).

And what if you're a small entrepreneur and need professional marketing help? Just click on Vendors. You'll find a list of folks who can help you with everything from Web design to mailing lists. But do me a favor. When you call them, tell them Bob Bly sent you. They're busy, too, and it helps if they know you're a qualified referral.

If prospects look up your topic on a search engine, will they find your site? There are 6 to 12 search engines that really count. You can and should manually register your site with Yahoo, Lycos, Alta Vista, Excite, Go, Netscape Search, AOL Search, MSN Search, Snap, HotBot, Google, and Infoseek. "If you want your site to be listed with search engines, pay your Web master to select the best candidates and make the submissions manually," writes Jonathan Ward in *The Business-to-Business Marketer* (August 1999, page 3).

DRIVE TRAFFIC TO YOUR WEB SITE

Paul Conderino, of Business & Legal Reports, offers the following suggestions for driving traffic to your Web site:

- ✔ Put your URL (uniform resource locator—Web site address) on all promotions—direct mail, catalogs, card decks, fax marketing, space advertising, press releases, invoices, and renewals.

- ✔ Use search engines. Write short, compelling title and description tags for each page. Focus on one keyword phrase and use this keyword phrase in keyword meta tag, title tag, description tag, headline, body copy, and alt tags.

- ✔ Encourage prospects to register with you to build your e-mail database. Offer a resource and document center, free demos, catalogs, samples, drawings, or e-mail newsletter.

- ✔ Consider testing banner ads. Try offering some of your content in exchange for a free banner ad.

- ✔ Link your site to other sites. Set a goal of submitting a certain number of link requests per week. Search on your keywords to identify the ranking sites and then submit to those. Consider associations, magazines, consultants, and complimentary sites.

- ✔ Build strategic partnerships and alliances. List your products on another company's site in exchange for a small royalty on any sales. Consider submitting articles for an e-mail newsletter in exchange for a Web link and additional promotion.

- ✔ Make it "sticky." Offer your prospects a reason to keep coming back. Good content, free resources and tools, contests/drawings work well.

You must give people a reason to visit your site. Internic reports that there are more than 1.5 million Internet sites. So why in the world should anyone take the time to see yours? If you have your picture there, or your brochure, or a cute saying, who cares? People care only about themselves. If you don't give them an appealing reason to zip over to your site, why complain if they don't visit it?

MONITORING AND MEASURING WEB SITE TRAFFIC

Have a guest page on your Web site. People who are prospects can fill out the page to request more information on your programs, get pricing, check your schedule and availability, or request other information. They in turn give you their contact information. You can also leave fields for them to answer other questions, such as whether they have a specific date in mind to hire you or what topic they want you to speak about. When the form is completed, they click a Submit button and their reply is e-mailed to you automatically for follow-up. A good measure of your Web site's effectiveness is how many qualified prospects complete your guest page online and what percentage of those become clients.

There are several services marketers use to measure Web site traffic:

StatMarket.com—*Internet statistics and user trends in real time.* Services include e-data mining. StatMarket.com presents raw data computed from millions of daily Internet visitors to Web sites monitored by WebSideStory Technology. StatMarket.com is the most accurate source of data on Internet user trends.

HitBOX.com—*Web site traffic counter and analysis tool.* HitBOX (and its high-end counterpart StatMarket eData Mining) remotely and anonymously collects and warehouses data from visitors to Web sites. In other words, it monitors the "who, what, when, and where" of every visit.

Hundreds of thousands of Web sites analyze their traffic with the HitBOX technology. Through the company's massive in-house network operating center, WebSideStory analyzes and stores data from billions of visitors to these sites every month. This has created an immense warehouse of data on Internet users—the largest of its kind. WebSideStory converts the massive amounts of raw Internet user data it collects into usable information.

On the guest page of your Web site, place a box that says "Click here if you are willing to receive e-mail messages of interest from time to time." Respondents who check off the box and then submit the form are said to have "opted in"— meaning they have given you (and anyone else you allow) permission to send promotional e-mail to them.

HitBOX.com is the most popular and comprehensive Web traffic analysis service and the largest listing of independent Web sites ranked by traffic.

INTERNET DIRECT MAIL

Effective speaker marketing means keeping in contact with prospects frequently. Sending a monthly or bimonthly e-mail to your opt-in prospects is an easy and inexpensive way to do this.

For instance, you might send a short e-mail newsletter (called an "e-zine") once a month. In addition, maybe once every other month you send a promotional message about a new seminar or course you offer. You can also update prospects, especially speakers bureaus, with your seminar schedule via e-mail.

Another option is to rent a mailing list of opt-in prospect names for a cold promotional mailing. As long as the names are opt-in, this is legal and is not considered spam (illegal "junk" e-mail).

Internet direct mail typically generates a response rate between 1 and 20 percent, although some do better and a few do worse. Since the copy in your e-mail plays a big role in whether your e-marketing message ends up at the bottom or the top of that range, here are some tips for writing effective Internet direct mail:

1. At the beginning of the e-mail, put a "From" line and a "Subject" line. The subject line should be constructed like a short attention-grabbing, curiosity-arousing outer envelope teaser, compelling recipients to read further—without being so blatantly promotional it turns them off. Example: "Come on back to Idea Forum!"

2. The e-mail from line identifies you as the sender if you're e-mailing to your house file. If you're e-mailing to a rented list,

the from line might identify the list owner as the sender. This is especially effective with opt-in lists where the list owner (e.g., a Web site) has a good relationship with its users.

3. Some e-marketers think the from line is trivial and unimportant; others think it's critical. Internet copywriter Ivan Levison says, "I often use the word 'Team' in the from line. It makes it sound as if there's a group of bright, energetic, enthusiastic people standing behind the product." For instance, if you are sending an e-mail to a rented list of computer people to promote a new software product, your subject and from lines might read as follows: From: The Adobe PageMill Team/Subject: Adobe PageMill 3.0 limited-time offer!

4. Despite the fact that "free" is a proven, powerful response-booster in traditional direct marketing, and that the Internet culture has a bias in favor of free offers rather than paid offers, some e-marketers avoid free in the subject line. The reason is the spam filter software some Internet users have installed to screen their e-mail. These filters eliminate incoming promotional e-mail, and many identify any message with free in the subject line as promotional.

5. Lead off the message copy with a killer headline or lead-in sentence. You need to get a terrific benefit right up front. Pretend you're writing envelope teaser copy or are writing a headline for a sales letter.

6. In the first paragraph, deliver a mini-version of your complete message. State the offer and provide an immediate response mechanism, such as clicking on a link connected to a Web page. This appeals to Internet prospects with short attention spans.

7. After the first paragraph, present expanded copy that covers the features, benefits, proof, and other information the buyer needs to make a decision. This appeals to the prospect who needs more details than a short paragraph can provide.

8. The offer and response mechanism should be repeated in the close of the e-mail, as in a traditional direct mail letter. But they should almost always appear at the very beginning, too. That way, busy Internet users who don't have time to read and who give each e-mail only a second or two get the whole story.

9. John Wright, of the Internet marketing services firm MediaSynergy, says that if you put multiple response links within your e-mail message, 95 percent of click-through responses will come

from the first two. Therefore, you should probably limit the number of click-through links in your e-mail to three. An exception might be an e-newsletter or e-zine broken into five or six short items, where each item is on a different subject and therefore each has its own link.

10. Use wide margins. You don't want to have weird wraps or breaks. Limit yourself to about 55 to 60 characters per line. If you think a line is going to be too long, insert a character return. Internet copywriter Joe Vitale sets his margins at 20 and 80, keeping sentence length to 60 characters and ensuring the whole line gets displayed on the screen without odd text breaks.

11. Take it easy on the all-caps. You can use words in all caps, but do so carefully. They can be a little hard to read—and in the world of e-mail, using all-caps gives the impression that you're shouting.

12. In general, shorter is better. This is not the case in classic mail-order selling, where as a general principle "the more you tell, the more you sell." E-mail is a unique environment. Readers are quickly sorting through a bunch of messages and aren't disposed to stick with you for a long time.

13. Regardless of length, get the important points across quickly. If you want to give a lot of product information, add it lower down in your e-mail message. You might also consider an attachment, such as a Word document, PDF file, or HTML page. People who need more information can always scroll down or click for it. The key benefits and deal should be communicated in the first screen, or very soon afterward.

14. The tone should be helpful, friendly, informative, and educational, not promotional or hard-sell. "Information is the gold in cyberspace," says Vitale. Trying to sell readers with a traditional hyped-up sales letter won't work. People online want information and lots of it. You'll have to add solid material to your puffed-up sales letter to make it work online. Refrain from saying your service is "the best" or that you offer "quality." Those are empty, meaningless phrases. Be specific. How are you the best? What exactly do you mean by quality? And who says it besides you? And even though information is the gold, readers don't want to be bored. They seek, like all of us, excitement. Give it to them.

15. Including an opt-out statement prevents flaming (angry replies) from recipients who feel they have been spammed. State that

Short statements that tease the reader, similar to "fascinations" in printed direct mail (e.g., "What never to eat on an airplane"), work well as subject lines in Internet direct mail. Example: "Advice from Bill Gates" is better than "Bill Gates on Innovation."

your intention is to respect their privacy, and make it easy for them to prevent further promotional e-mails from being sent to them. All they have to do is click on Reply and type "Unsubscribe" or "Remove" in the subject line. Example: "We respect your online time and privacy, and pledge not to abuse this medium. If you prefer not to receive further e-mails from us of this kind, please reply to this e-mail and type 'Remove' in the subject line."

Chapter

Contracts, Letters of Agreement, Fees, Terms

T he final step in getting a speaking assignment is to firm up the deal and get the paperwork written and signed. It's also nice to have a deposit check that has cleared in your business bank account.

What are the critical details at this stage? They include seven areas:

1. *How much money you are getting and when it is to be paid.* What is the speaking fee? Do you get paid in advance? Many speakers get half up front, the balance paid after delivery of the talk. Some speakers insist that the client give them a check for the balance *at the presentation*, but I just bill them for the balance owed after the talk: I don't want to have my hand out and appear to be focused on the fee rather than the audience, client, and event.

If the client is a well-known local company, a Fortune 500 corporation, or a major national association, I might be willing to simply bill the entire fee upon completion, if the client asks. But it's better to get half your fee up front. This shows a serious commitment and ensures you get paid if the engagement is canceled for some reason.

Be clear on what else you are providing for the fee. Are handouts and visuals included, or is there an extra charge for them? Traditionally speakers supply their own handouts and visuals, although some charge for extensive handouts bound into workbooks.

At times you may accept a free or low-fee engagement for self-promotion or other reasons. In these agreements, I make clear that I consider this pro bono (charity) work and I reserve the right to cancel if I am offered an engagement at my regular fee. (I will of course do a presentation for the group I am canceling at another date, if they wish.) This avoids getting into the situation of having to turn down a good speaking engagement because you committed the date to something not as lucrative or worthwhile.

2. *Expenses the client will cover.* My usual arrangement is that all travel and lodging expenses, including airfare, hotel, meals, and ground transportation, are paid by the client. Some speakers prefer to buy their own airline tickets and let the clients reimburse them, so the frequent flier miles accrue to the speaker. But many associations and corporations prefer to purchase the ticket and send it to you, because their corporate travel departments get better rates. I do whatever the client wants.

Some clients with limited budgets may not want to cover certain expenses, or they may want to limit these expenses to a fixed dollar amount. For instance, one conference company said it would pay for my hotel and airline ticket, but limit my other expenses to a total of $150 a day. Be careful about saying yes too quickly to such an arrangement. Find out approximately how much those other expenses will be before you accept.

3. *The services and products you are providing for the fee.* I specify in my agreement the length and hours of the presentation, and whether handouts are provided. Some conference and association clients ask but do not insist that speakers be present for the entire event, not just their session. Since time is money, I usually will not agree to this, and will spell out in my agreement that my client should expect me just for my session only.

4. *The date, hours, and size of audience.* What date is the program? What time—the morning or the afternoon? I prefer morning, because I can fly out and get back to my office or home at a reasonable hour that day.

Be clear about the length and hours. Several times, I have been hired to do a 90-minute speech, only to see on the conference program that my session is two hours long. Imagine my panic at suddenly having to come up with another half hour of material! Many association and corporate clients seem amazingly unaware that, to the speaker, there is a big difference between a seven-hour and a six-hour class, or a 90-minute versus a 60-minute speech.

Put in the contract the estimated size of the group. Some speakers charge more for extra attendees, and if this is your policy, the rate per extra attendee above the agreed-upon limit should also be spelled out.

5. *Cancellation policy.* What if the event is canceled—does the client owe you any money? Many speakers say there is no penalty if they are able to book another program for that day; otherwise, the client pays a kill fee. The kill fee should be presented to the client in writing and incorporated as part of the agreement.

My cancellation policy is as follows: Client pays all noncancelable expenses incurred such as airfare, reproduction of handouts, and so on—no matter what. As for my fee, the client pays 10 percent if they cancel after signing a contract regardless of how far in advance; 25 percent if they cancel less than eight weeks in advance; and 50 percent if they cancel less than four weeks in advance.

6. *Ancillary product sales.* If you have negotiated the right to sell your products at the event, this should be spelled out in the contract. If the client gets a cut, this percentage should be specified.

One problem is: Who will sit at the table where the products are displayed and take the orders? Often the association will provide a volunteer to do this for free, especially if you ask. Pay the volunteer with a gift of your most expensive product.

7. *Taping rights.* My recommended terms for taping your program are as follows: The client can tape you and offer the tape to its members. If the tape is free, you get nothing. If the client sells it, you get a 10 percent royalty. You retain copyright and reproduction rights to the material, and you are given a copy of the tape at no cost.

Put all of this in writing and get the client to sign it. You can use a contract form as shown in Appendix F. Or you can draft a simple letter of agreement for the client's signature, as shown:

November 10, 2000

Mr. Gage Johnson
Regional Claims Manager
Dean & Homer
340 Pine Street
San Francisco, CA 94104

Dear Gage,

I'm delighted with the prospect of working with you on our upcoming "Effective Business Writing for Insurance Professionals" program.

The next few paragraphs spell out our agreement:

The Communication Workshop agrees to provide a one-day program in "Effective Business Writing for Insurance Professionals" on January 24, 2000, from 9:00 A.M. to 4:00 P.M. The

Workshop also agrees to review responses to our needs assessment, "The Claims/Underwriting Audit," in advance of our classes. We will also collect and review writing samples in preparation for the classes.

Dean & Homer agrees to pay The Communication Workshop a fee of _____ for the seminar (plus expenses) for the training of as many as 15 participants in the seminar. Additional participants are billable at $175 each. The fee includes all pre-course work, course handouts, copies of my book, *The Elements of Business Writing*, for each participant, one year's access to our Writing Hotline following the training, and three months' access to our fax/e-mail editorial service.

If this is agreeable, please sign and return a copy of this letter. I've included 15 copies of "The Claims/Underwriting Audit" and ask that you distribute a copy to each participant. Audits should be completed by the participants and returned to the Workshop, along with one or two writing samples per participant, by January 3, 2000. Some of the samples, with names deleted, will be critiqued during the seminar.

I'm looking forward to making this workshop both lively and productive.

Sincerely,

Gary Blake, Ph.D.

Signed _____ Date _____

Put the signed contract in your files. If you require a payment in advance, get that check too. Corporate chains of command can hold up paperwork and checks, but be wary of the client who is evasive when it comes to getting signed contracts and advance payments to you. A legitimate client with a real event should have no problem with your request for a written agreement and advance payment.

I have always operated on a very simple principle. People I like and who like me aren't going to cheat me in any way.
—Isaac Asimov, *Yours, Isaac Asimov* (Doubleday)

ACCEPTING CREDIT CARDS
ELIMINATES PAYMENT PROBLEMS

One tactic I use to eliminate payment delays and excuses is to tell clients they can charge my services to their credit card right over the phone. It's easy and convenient for customers, and that makes it more likely for them to order.

Mediamark Research reports that the average age of credit card holders in the United States is 45.6 years. Of 220 million Americans, 144 million have Visa, 93 million have MasterCard, 41 million have Discover, and 25 million have American Express, reports an article in *Upfront* newsletter. According to the article, having a merchant account can increase your sales volume 30 to 200 percent.

The only problem is that it's hard for some small businesses, particularly independent speakers, to gain the ability to accept credit cards. Banks are very reluctant to authorize credit card acceptance, mainly because they have been burned too many times by fraudulent businesses.

So, many businesses go on accepting only checks or money orders for payment, and miss out on the added sales they would get through credit cards. There is a way, though, for businesses that can't get bank authorization to accept credit cards.

If you have a long-term good relationship with your bank, that gives you some powerful leverage. Be willing to use that leverage to get what you want. After all, banks are in business for the same reason as the rest of us—to serve their customers and to make a profit.

As mentioned, the major credit cards in this country are Visa, MasterCard, Discover, and American Express. If your business caters to certain market segments, you may want to consider other types of credit cards. For example, if many of your customers are Japanese, you probably want to accept orders from JCB (Japan Credit Bureau) cardholders.

For European customers, consider Diners Club. You might also want to think about Carte Blanche cards.

To get established as a Visa and MasterCard merchant, start with your own bank. If you have a good relationship with it, it is your best bet. Another option you may want to add is American Express. The company is easy to deal with, and seems to have no bias against the Internet businesses.

The typical American Express cardholder has an affluent lifestyle and high household income, and is an impulsive buyer. Many businesses give their employees American Express credit cards for travel and other business expenses. So if you are selling products or services to businesspeople, by all means call American Express for a merchant account application.

A suggestion when you fill out your merchant account applications, whether it be for your bank, American Express, or whomever, is to be truthful, but give them as high an average per-order dollar figure as you can. They like to see average orders of $20 or more.

Higher average orders and higher sales volumes can reduce the percentage of each sale you will pay to the credit card issuer. This fee can vary anywhere from 1.5 percent to 5 percent, depending on your average size order, sales volume, and other factors. But even if you have to pay 5 percent, it's well worth it.

The easiest way to get a merchant account is to work with an independent sales organization (ISO), which acts as an intermediary between small businesses and banks. Appendix I lists a number of ISOs.

The ISOs will charge an additional fee for each transaction, so you will be paying a bit more than the standard percentage charged for credit card transactions. There will also be an application fee. Here are the typical charges to expect, as of this writing.

- ✔ *Application fees.* Usually, these range from $95 to $400 and may or may not be refundable.

- ✔ *Point of sale terminal purchase or lease.* The terminal you use to process the charge and check for fraudulent numbers is usually available from a bank for around $300, but you will be able to get this price only if a bank authorizes you. If working through an ISO, prices will range from $400 to even as high as $1,500. You can usually lease the terminal, though, at an average of $45 per month. The best thing to do is to find an ISO that will provide computer software that can be used in place of a terminal. This will usually cost only around $150.

- ✔ *Service fees.* Banks charge between 2 and 5 percent for processing a credit card purchase. ISOs charge more, usually 3 to 7 percent. They also usually charge a per-transaction fee of 20 to 25 cents, and a monthly statement fee of $5 to $10.

Why all these fees? Since ISOs want to work with only legitimate businesses and ones that will stay with them for a long period of time, if a business can afford these fees it is considered less of a risk. Thus, the important thing to do is to shop around for an ISO. Get as much information as you can about each ISO you are considering, and study it thoroughly. Look for hidden charges and unreasonable requirements.

Walter Chrysler, founder of the company that bears his name, was an accomplished auto mechanic. In fact, he started Chrysler only after buying a competitor's car, then taking it apart and putting it back together over 40 times until he was convinced he could make a better car at a lower cost.

When Walter saw a stranded motorist, he would pull up, bolt from his own car, and fix their motor in a jiffy. He would then hand them one of his business cards and express the hope of seeing them become his customers in the future.

—Peter Hay, *The Book of Business Anecdotes* (Wings Books)

All of these services will require you to fill out an application. Be totally truthful with everything on the application, and don't let the representative talk you into putting anything else down.

The reason is, if the banks affiliated with the ISO you use were to find out that any information on your application is false, you would probably be immediately canceled and your business name and address would go on a blacklist. This would prevent you from being able to accept credit cards for an indefinite period of time. Don't let this happen to you.

Most of the ISOs out there are legitimate, but there are a few that may put down spurious information rather than lose the fees they'd receive. Be sure to look everything over twice. If you do, you'll probably find an ISO that will work with you to expand your business through the acceptance of credit cards. See Appendix I for a list of credit card companies where you can apply for merchant status.

13

The 4 R's: Making Money from Referrals, Repeat Business, Reprints, and Resales

Getting people actually to hire you to give talks is a breakthrough, but it is only the first step. Your ongoing success is dependent on getting positive evaluations from audiences and clients, repeat business, and referrals. Achieving all of these things is covered in this chapter, including:

✔ How to design and conduct your program so your attendees can't help giving you excellent evaluations.

✔ How to design an evaluation form that helps you get additional business.

✔ How to get clients to hire you again and again.

✔ How to get clients to refer you to their colleagues for speaking assignments.

✔ How to maximize your income from the presentations you create.

Think of your speech not as a speech, but as a product. The more times you can sell the basic product, the more money you make from it.

This includes the same product in the same format to different audiences; the same product (a speech) in different formats (a college class, a corporate training seminar, an audiocassette album, a book); different versions of the product/topic (selling, selling financial services, selling annuities); and different levels of the product (selling, advanced selling, selling for nonsalespeople).

REFERRALS

The easiest way to get new clients is through referrals from existing clients, prospects, colleagues, and even competitors. Yet asking for referrals is often neglected in favor of other marketing techniques such as cold calling, letter writing, and proposals.

"Without question, selling through referrals is the most powerful way to build your business, not to mention the most enjoyable," writes sales trainer Bill Cates in his book *Unlimited Referrals* (Wheaton, MD: Thunder Hill Press). "Your buyers would rather meet you through a referral. The endorsement and testimony of others make them feel more comfortable opening their door to you and giving you their business."

How do you go about getting referrals? You do it by calling your best customers and asking them for referrals.

Although this can be a separate call, it's better if combined with a call for another purpose—to keep in touch, check on customer satisfaction, follow up on a job you submitted, or check on the status of a project. Here's how it might go:

> *You:* Mike, can I ask you a question?
>
> *Client:* Sure, go ahead.
>
> *You:* You seem pretty satisfied with the work I have done for you. Am I right?
>
> *Client:* Yes, very.
>
> *You:* Would you be comfortable recommending my speaking services to colleagues of yours who are not direct competitors with your firm?
>
> *Client:* Of course.
>
> *You:* Which of these people could I get in touch with to let them know about my program and how it can help them?
>
> *Client:* Joe Doakes at Hummingbird Industries.
>
> *You:* And do you have Joe's phone number?

Client: Yes, here it is.

You: Joe Doakes at Hummingbird. May I use your name when I call him?

Client: Certainly.

You: Great. I'll call Joe. Who else do you know who might be able to benefit from our services?

You then repeat the cycle—ending with "And who else?"—until your client gives you all the referrals he or she is going to give you right now. By asking "And who else?" you will probably get two or three referrals instead of the one the customer was going to give you. Three is probably the limit for one call—clients will run out of ready names and get tired of giving the referrals—but ask until they say, "That's it."

I recommend you send a thank-you note to customers who give you referrals. A small, tasteful gift is optional. (I send a copy of one of my books.)

Keep the customer up-to-date if anything comes from the referral. If you get business out of it, send another thank-you and a slightly better gift (my choices are a gift basket of muffins from Wolferman's—800-999-1910—or one of your expensive videotape programs).

You can ask these same customers for more referrals later on. Just don't do it too frequently. Once every four or five months seems about right. If you do something particularly good for them, such as solve a problem or complete a successful project, by all means ask for a reference as you bask in the glow of their praise.

REPEAT ORDERS

Most speakers concentrate on new business. Here's how to win lucrative ongoing repeat business from existing clients. Repeat assignments are eas-

Don't neglect *internal* referrals: getting someone you know in an organization to refer you to the training buyer. Executives are often more willing to see you if the referral is from someone in their own organization than from someone outside.

ier to get and take less time to prepare for, since you are already familiar with the audience and their needs.

Because many salespeople love the thrill of the chase, and because they often get bigger commissions for bringing in new customers, soliciting repeat sales and reorders from active accounts is often ignored at the expense of pursuing new business.

Not every salesperson makes this mistake. Stockbrokers, for example, know the value of working existing accounts. If you have an account with a brokerage, you get frequent calls from your broker offering new ideas for companies he or she wants you to invest in. But salespeople in some other industries are not as savvy. For example, the company that sold me my computer has never contacted me to offer any upgrades or new services, despite the fact that it sells many I would want—a bigger memory, better CD-ROM drive, higher-resolution laser printer, DSL modems, or home page design. A mistake? I think so.

Have a plan for periodically recontacting active customers to remind them of your existence and give them news of any special offers, discounts, new services, or new ideas for training programs they might benefit from. Doing so will substantially increase reorders and repeat sales from your database of existing clients.

In particular, let existing customers know of new services you are offering, such as Internet-based training or self-paced courses on CD-ROM. This cross-selling will get existing customers to give you assignments they would have never thought to call you for before.

Experience shows that an active customer is 5 to 10 times more likely to buy something from you than a prospect you cold call from a prospecting directory or telemarketing list. That means working your database can yield 5 to 10 times the response of a new business or customer acquisition effort aimed at a similar number of prospects.

How frequently should you keep in touch with existing customers? It's different for every business, but for speakers, a contact every quarter—a call or mailing once every three months, for a total of four in a given year—makes sense. It's frequent enough so the customer doesn't forget about you, but infrequent enough so that you're not pestering customers or spending an inordinate amount of time and money making these contacts.

If possible, make some of the contacts phone calls. You can increase frequency of contact by adding one, two, or three mailings a year or by substituting a mailing for one of the regular four annual phone calls. The mailing need not be elaborate. Remember, this is just to keep in touch and keep your name before the customer. A simple postcard or short sales letter is sufficient.

It costs 5 to 10 times more to make a first sale to a new customer than to make a repeat sale to an existing customer.

"Seek a reason to keep in touch with your existing clients so they don't fall into a dormant cycle," writes Loriann Oberlin in her book *Writing for Money* (Writer's Digest Books). "It takes much less effort to sell a previously satisfied client on a new job than a customer unfamiliar with your work. Send correspondence and clippings your clients might appreciate and schedule lunch meetings periodically to discuss your client's changing needs."

REPRINTS AND TAPES

I earn an extra $5,000 to $10,000 each year selling photocopied reprints of published articles I've written, copies of my out-of-print books, and audio- and videocassette recordings of my speeches and seminars, all via mail order. You can, too. Here's how:

1. Whenever possible, make sure you maintain reproduction and mail order rights to all your works. When I am taped at a conference or seminar, I allow it on condition that I retain the copyright and distribution rights to the presentation. I also require a copy of the tape be given to me.

2. Get extra tear sheets of published articles. Store in hanging files. Number each file. Keep a master index so you can easily look up and retrieve any piece by its code number. Make and store multiple copies of each piece. Copies should be of high quality with no blurs or smudges, and easy to read.

3. Buy extra copies of your books from your publishers. When the book goes out of print, buy the remainders and store them in your house, if you have the room.

4. If you are a guest on a radio or TV show, get a tape master of your appearance. Before accepting the engagement, inform the producer that in exchange for appearing on the show, you maintain duplication rights.

5. If you give a talk where you will not be taped, arrange to have a professional videotape or audiotape it at your expense.

6. Take these tapes to a duplicator and have copies made with neat-looking but inexpensive laser labels. I use Dove Enterprises in Cuyahoga Falls, Ohio (800-233-3683). Use a numbering system and make a master list of tapes with numbers and titles.

7. Make sure your contact information, including name, address, and phone number, appears on everything you write or produce. Solicit reader feedback by asking for questions, comments, and suggestions. Encourage readers to contact you for more information or to establish a dialogue on your topic.

Soon you will have a line of information products—article reprints, books, audiocassettes, videotapes—that you have written or presented. You will also find yourself receiving frequent queries from readers who have questions or want to buy additional books and other materials you have written.

The greatest profit opportunity for selling these information products to your readers is through a mini-catalog. A good example is my Resource Guide shown in Appendix F. As you can see, the catalog lists article reprints, books, and tapes including title, description, and price. It also includes a coupon the reader can use to order items.

Such a catalog need not be elaborate. You can print it in black ink on white or colored paper. You don't need to illustrate it with drawings or photos.

One of these mini-catalogs should be included in every outgoing order you ship to your mail order customers. The beauty is that it promotes your entire product line at virtually no cost—there is no postage or envelope to pay for, since it is mailed with the product shipment. The only cost is the few pennies per catalog for printing.

For a small home-based business selling information products by mail, including a mini-catalog in all product shipments can double your annual gross sales or better, with no added marketing cost.

You can promote your information products in other ways, of course. For instance, you can periodically mail your mini-catalog or other special offers to your list of mail order customers. But the cheapest, easiest way to sell back-end products is by enclosing mini-catalogs with products being shipped and sending them to anyone and everyone who writes, calls, or e-mails you. If you don't do this, you are missing out on a large share of the profits your writing business can generate for you.

On one occasion I gave a 90-minute talk on direct mail to a direct

Retain the rights to the printed and spoken material you create. Put a copyright notation (see the back of the title page of this book for an example) on everything you produce. Keep computer files of all material for easy reformatting and reuse in multiple applications.

marketing association. I retained the rights and got a master of the tape. Within a few months, a client in the direct marketing industry ordered 5,000 copies of the tape from me to use as a premium. Had I not retained the rights, that check would have been written to the association. Instead, it was written to me, at a profit of thousands of dollars.

Reprint Sales Inc. actively markets reprints for publishers and others with information they own the copyright to. For information, contact RSI, 60 East 42 Street, #3810, New York, New York 10165, phone 800-567-7706.

RESALES

Never create a program that you only do once. If you customize a program for a client, create a generic version (eliminating anything proprietary you created for the client, of course) and sell that to other firms with similar training needs.

Consider creating versions of your programs that corporations can license from you. For the client that wants to train thousands of employees in your area of expertise, it might be better and more cost-effective for the company to have its own in-house trainers give your course rather than bring you in so many times. You create workbooks and a teacher's guide for the trainers, including camera-ready handout masters they can reproduce with their photocopier or reprographics department.

You get a fee—maybe one-tenth or one-quarter of what your fee would be if you conducted the session personally—for each time the course is presented. The customer saves on your travel expenses and the majority of your fee. You in turn earn passive income, getting paid whenever the course is given, even though you are not doing the presentation yourself.

When you have such a reproducible course in a binder and with workbooks so trainers other than you can give it, you can also franchise

Carol Andrus, a freelance writer, once sold and resold a single article she wrote to 67 different publications. Her total revenues for that one article were $33,000.

your program. Other trainers can buy the rights to give the presentation, using your materials. You could charge a flat franchise fee, a per-presentation fee, or some combination.

EVALUATIONS

The higher your evaluations, the more pleased the clients are, and the more likely they will be to hire you again. Here is a technique for improving your evaluation ratings taught to me by speaker Rob Gilbert.

About two-thirds of the way through the allotted time, ask students to rate you so far on a scale of 1 to 10, 10 being the greatest seminar they ever heard, and 1 being an utter waste of their time. They can write this down but should not show it to you.

Then ask them to write down what questions you would have to answer, what they would have to learn, or what else you would have to cover that would get them to rate you a 9 or 10 if they have not already done so.

Next, go around the room and ask them to share the questions or concerns with you. Discuss them during the remainder of the seminar.

Then give out the evaluation forms to be completed. Even if the attendees weren't wild about your class, they will feel compelled to rate you higher than they otherwise would have. After all, you asked them what it would take to rate you higher. So they reason that if they didn't ask it, and you didn't cover it, they and not you are to blame—which, if you use this technique as a teaching tool and not just a gimmick, is in fact true.

Every transaction is an opportunity to confirm or dash customer expectations and thereby reinforce or destroy trust.

—Ron Zemke, Performance Research Associates

What others say about you and your product, service, or business is at least 1,000% more convincing than what you say, even though you are 1,000% more eloquent.
—Dan Kennedy, *No B.S. Selling* (Self-Counsel Press)

EVALUATION FORMS

Use the model evaluation form in Appendix F, or create one that you like better.

The important thing is to distribute and collect evaluation forms at as many of your sessions as will allow it. If the sponsor doesn't do evaluation forms, it may simply be because it doesn't have one. So bring copies of your own form and offer it to the sponsor. Most will be thrilled that you did.

Give out the evaluation forms five minutes before the session is up, not at the very last second. That way, people will take the time to fill them out before rushing to their next session. Have someone other than you collect the forms. If attendees see you collect them, they may be embarrassed to write negative comments for fear that you will know they personally criticized you.

The sample evaluation form asks them to say, in their own words, what they liked about you and your program. The form also contains a release that says you have the right to reprint their comments in your marketing materials. You collect testimonials you can use on your Web site, in your brochures, and in presentations to potential clients.

Boosting Your Speaking Income with Information Products

S peakers and seminar leaders package their expertise and information in ways other than speaking to groups on a per diem basis.

On-site speeches and seminars are to some degree customized for the client, but not all clients can afford or even want customized advice. A less costly way for you to sell—and for clients to acquire—your information is to package it in standardized, noncustomized formats. This information can be sold at a lower cost than one-on-one consulting, and since it is not proprietary or customized, the same information can be sold to multiple buyers—more than you would have time to work with in person. This chapter shows how to create and sell such information products to your clients and others.

If you charge $1,000 a day to speak, your maximum speaking income for today is $1,000. But if you sell an audio album of that same speech for $50, you can make $2,000 by selling 40 albums today. If you sell 400 albums, you can make $20,000 in just one day. The income potential in products, unlike services, is not limited by your time, which is finite.

WHAT ARE INFORMATION PRODUCTS?

Information products are printed, recorded, or electronic files containing prewritten information sold at a per-unit price. Information products is a broad term referring to everything from pamphlets, special reports, books, audiocassettes, videos, newsletters, and fax advisory services to CD-ROMs, software, and computer-based training.

Information products present in-depth data, information, or discussion of a topic related to the speaker or seminar leader's area of expertise. One speaker and seminar leader specializing in ISO 9000 compliance, for example, offers as an information product a boilerplate-quality manual on a disk. The boilerplate can easily be customized to a client's operation, eliminating the time and effort of writing the quality manual entirely from scratch. Another information product produced by this ISO speaker and seminar leader is a mini-directory of firms certified to perform ISO audits.

Traditionally, speakers and seminar leaders have offered booklets (because they are inexpensive and easy to produce) and books (because of the prestige and credibility). But with the growth of the Internet, many prospects like to buy information in electronic form, whether as downloads from a Web site or on a CD-ROM or computer disk.

This actually works to your advantage as an information seller: You can package essentially the same information in multiple media, and sell it many times over. Not only will different people buy information in different formats, but some customers will actually pay for the same information several times over to get it in different formats!

One speaker asked me, "What are the criteria for a marketable information product at a time when we are all suffering from information overload?" The answer: Information products provide specific and detailed answers to questions and problems in narrow niche subjects not usually addressed by newspapers, magazines, and general media. As Richard Saul Wurman observes in his book *Information Anxiety* (Doubleday), "The information explosion has backfired, leaving us inundated

Speakers can make more money by selling information products. But being the author of a book or other information product can also help you get more speaking engagements.

with facts but starved for understanding." Information products cut through the clutter, providing clients with the precise information they want in a minimum of words.

REASONS WHY SPEAKERS AND SEMINAR LEADERS SHOULD PRODUCE INFORMATION PRODUCTS

The main reasons why speakers and seminar leaders should produce and offer information products, and why Howard Shenson said, "Publishing is every speaker or seminar leader's second business," are as follows:

✔ Being published builds credibility. The highest-paid speakers and seminar leaders are typically those who have written best-selling books in their fields.

✔ Information products let clients sample your information before they hire you. Once, the marketing director at a computer company said to me, "I am considering several speakers and seminar leaders for teaching direct marketing to our staff; why should I choose you over them?" I sent him my book on direct marketing with a note that said, "If this doesn't convince you, hire someone else." I got the job and a large client that I've been working with for years on numerous projects.

✔ Information products give you an advantage over the competition. If you have written a book or produced an audio album and your competitor hasn't, this gives you an edge in winning contracts.

✔ Information products allow you profitably to serve that segment of the market that can't or won't hire you for private consultation. Instead of turning away prospects who can't afford you, you can offer them a lower-priced alternative: an information product that delivers much of the same advice you would give in a private consultation. In this way, leads you've paid to generate that you'd otherwise have to turn down flat can become product buyers, producing additional income for you.

✔ Writing books, booklets, and articles sharpens your thinking, forces you to organize your information more logically, and builds your own expertise in your subject area. Creating information products helps you become a better speaker or seminar leader.

Being the author of information products builds your reputation as an expert in your field. "The reverence people have for the printed word is amazing," writes Edward Uhlan in his book *The Rogue of Publishers' Row* (Exposition Press). "Simply because a man appears in print, the public assumes he has something authoritative to say."

TIPS FOR PRODUCING SPECIFIC TYPES OF INFORMATION PRODUCTS

As discussed in Chapter 2, many speakers and seminar leaders write books. Not only does the book promote your consulting practice, but you can generate additional revenue from book sales. If you cannot find a publisher for a book, you can always self-publish it. A 200-page book will sell for $10 to $30 or higher. The more specialized the book, the higher the price. Costs for producing a self-published book are presented in Table 14.1.

Although they complement one another rather than compete, learning through books in some ways has distinct advantages over the seminars and speeches we give. As writer Jerry Buchanan points out:

> A book that instructs in some profitable field is a priceless treasure. It stands patient and mute until you command it to teach. When it teaches, it teaches only as fast as you are capable of

TABLE 14.1 Costs for Producing a Self-Published Book	
Item	*Cost*
Proofreader	$12/hour
Copyeditor	$15/hour
Indexer	$2/page
Front cover design	$800–$1,200
Typesetting	$6–$10/page
Printing of 5,000 copies of 224-page book	$1.20–$1.30/copy
Printing of a four-color cover, 5,000 copies	$1,200–$2,800

Source: "What Should Things Cost?" by Curt Matthews, *PMA Newsletter*, March 1997.

learning, and will repeat the difficult parts as often as is necessary to firmly entrench them in your brain. It will never rebuke you for tardiness to class, nor complain under a thousand interruptions. It never forgets even a minor principle of its conceptual message, yet it will not scold you if you forget even major ones. Such a book ranks with a faithful hound as one of man's best friends. If the bookseller offers it and you pass up the chance of ownership, who suffers the most: You? Or the bookseller, who will only sell it to the next one who browses?

Here is a quick overview of some other popular formats for information products, along with suggestions on producing each:

✔ *Tip sheets.* Tip sheets are short, to-the-point fact sheets on a particular subject. They are usually printed on one or two sides of an 8½-by-11-inch sheet of paper. Advice or information is typically (but not necessarily) presented as a series of short, numbered items or tips. You can write tip sheets as electronic files, then run them off one at a time on your laser printer as orders come in. You can also e-mail tip sheets to clients who prefer an electronic file. I typically charge $1 to $2 for a tip sheet.

✔ *Booklets and pamphlets.* These are, in essence, expanded versions of tip sheets. They contain similar information except in more detail: In a booklet, there's space to flesh out each point more fully. Booklets are generally four by nine inches, so they can be mailed in a standard #10 business envelope. A booklet is constructed by printing and folding the pages and then saddle-stitching them together (saddle-stitching is binding by stapling through the fold). Booklets typically run anywhere from 8 to 16 pages, although they can be longer. I price booklets at $5 to $12 each.

✔ *Special reports.* This format is typically longer than a booklet, and so can be even more detailed. Special reports, like tip sheets, are printed on 8½-by-11-inch sheets of paper, but are multiple pages instead of one page. The larger page format allows for bigger illustrations, tables, and charts than you can put in a booklet. A special report can run anywhere from 5 pages to 100 or more, although typically they are 6 to 12 pages. I desktop publish the master pages, then run off copies of the report on my office copier, collate, and staple them. For a 10-page special report, I charge $6 to $10 or higher.

✔ *Monographs.* A monograph is an essay or article on a single subject. They are similar in look and feel to special reports, but often on the lengthy side (20 to 30 pages) and written in more formal, professional language. The medical products industry frequently uses monographs written by doctors to promote a drug, material, instrument, or piece of equipment. They give monographs away free, but you can charge $5 to $25 or more for a well-written monograph on a topic of interest to your prospects.

✔ *Resource guides.* These are mini-directories of information resources in a particular field—for example, Web sites for quality control professionals. A resource guide of five or six pages might sell for $5 to $8.

✔ *Manuals.* Reference manuals are long, comprehensive special reports, usually placed in a binder or notebook and organized into sections. Manuals can range from 30 to 150 pages or more. Prices can range from $10 to $50 or higher.

✔ *Audiotapes.* Audiocassettes are a popular medium for disseminating spoken-word business and how-to information. A single audiocassette is easy to produce. Just get a speaking engagement, and tape your talk. Then make duplicates, put a nice label on them, and sell the tapes. A single audiocassette retails for between $10 and $15. Duplication costs for small quantities are $1 to $2 each, depending on packaging. Appendix E lists vendors who can tape and duplicate talks for you. Some organizations routinely tape speaker presentations and sell them to their members. You should make it a condition that you retain the rights to the tape and get a free master copy. This eliminates the cost of paying a professional or buying your own taping equipment.

✔ *Audio albums.* Once you have done eight, six, or even two tapes on related topics, you can package them in a vinyl album jacket and sell them as an audiocassette program. A six-cassette album can sell for $49 to $79. Album jackets are a couple of dollars each, and available from any tape duplication service.

✔ *Power packs.* A power pack is a multimedia information product. Typically, it's a combination of tapes, reports, and perhaps a book or CD-ROM, all in a nice package. Power packs can sell for $50 to $150 or more.

✔ *Videotapes.* You can videotape your presentation, duplicate it, and sell the videos. The video should be edited professionally in a video studio. Add graphics, special effects, charts, and other

> The late seminar leader and consultant Howard Shenson
> told me that he often did a public seminar only once, and
> solely for the purpose of videotaping the performance and
> turning it into a video album he would then sell by mail. He
> said it was much more profitable to sell a program on tape
> than do it live again and again.

footage for a varied presentation that's more than just you talking behind a lectern. Have a nice label or package. A single video can sell for $29 to $59 or more.

✔ *Paid-subscription newsletter.* Some speakers and seminar leaders produce a quarterly promotional newsletter of four to eight pages they distribute free to prospects and clients. Make your newsletter meatier (more information; no self-promotion), longer (six to eight pages), and more frequent (monthly), and you can charge a subscription fee ranging from $29 to $249 a year or more.

✔ *Software.* If some of the processes you teach can be automated using software, consider working with a software developer to create custom software that you can sell to your clients and attendees. As mentioned, one consultant who gives workshops on how to write documentation for ISO compliance sells a disk containing boilerplate text and outlines for all the necessary documents she helps attendees create in her class.

HOW TO SELL YOUR PRODUCTS PROFITABLY TO CLIENTS AND PROSPECTS

You can get significant additional income with virtually no extra marketing cost by selling information products to clients and prospects.

Include your bounce-back catalog in the packets of information you send to potential clients. Many, even if they don't hire you, will place an order for information products. Those who do become further educated in your expertise—and are more likely to hire you.

Periodically remail catalogs to all leads who do not become clients. Many will place orders for your information products.

For those prospects whose business you actively seek, you can impress them by sending some of your information products, free, as an enticement to hire you and as a demonstration of your expertise. Books,

Speaker and consultant Dr. Jeffrey Lant says, "A book is a brochure that will never be thrown away."

booklets, article reprints, and monographs are more interesting than sales brochures alone and more likely to make the impression you want: that of the knowledgeable authority in your field.

I give away dozens of audiocassettes, article reprints, and full-length books each year to those prospects I want to become clients. It pays off handsomely. What's neat is that the information product has a high perceived value—that of the price listed on its cover and in your catalog. But it costs you only a fraction of that amount to produce and give away. And while a brochure might get lost in a file folder, a book sits on the prospect's shelf where he or she can always see it and therefore be continually reminded of you and your expertise.

HOW TO USE DIRECT MARKETING TO BOOST YOUR PRODUCT SALES

Is the information explosion a good thing for information marketers? Actually, it's a mixed blessing:

- ✔ People have too much to read and not enough time to read it.
- ✔ More and more information is competing for their attention.
- ✔ There is a proliferation of low-cost/no-cost information sources eating into the market for your expensive information products.

Fortunately, you can still succeed in selling information by mail. It's tougher than it was in yesteryear, I think. So here are eight rules and guidelines formulated specifically for information marketers competing in the Information Age:

1. *Narrow the focus.* Although the most profitable product may be one with wide appeal, such as Joe Karbo's *Lazy Man's Way to Riches* or Bob Kalian's *A Few Thousand of the Best Free Things in America*, goldmine concepts such as these are difficult to come by. Today we live in an age of specialization. People have narrow, specific areas of interest and eagerly seek the best information in these niche areas. Match your own interests and consulting expertise with the information needs of an identifiable market, and you're on your way.

How big must this market be? Jerry Buchanan, publisher of *Towers Club Newsletter*, a how-to newsletter for information marketers and self-publishers, says that "any group large enough that some publisher has seen fit to publish a magazine about them or for them" is large enough for your purposes.

2. *Seize a subject.* The tendency of the typical magazine writer or book author is to wander from subject to subject to satisfy a never-ending curiosity about all things. But the speaker or seminar leader, an information marketer, must behave differently. He or she must latch onto a narrow niche or topic, make it his or her own, and produce a *series* of information products that meets the needs of information-seekers buying materials on this subject. Not only does this increase profits by giving you more products to offer your customers, it also helps establish you as a recognized expert and authority in your field.

3. *Plan the "back end" before you start marketing.* Many entrepreneurial direct-response advertisers dream of duplicating the one-shot success of Joe Karbo and of getting rich from a single mail-order book. But it rarely happens. This "front end," or first sale, *can* be profitable, if cost-effective marketing techniques are used. But the real profits are in the back end—selling a related line of additional information products to repeat customers.

I advise you to come up with and plan this back end of related products *before* launching a direct response campaign. Otherwise, precious opportunities for repeat sales will be lost if you can offer only a single product to eager, information-hungry buyers.

4. *Test your concept with classified ads.* Most information marketers want to immediately mail thousands of direct mail packages or place full-page ads.

That's fine if you can afford to risk $5,000 to $25,000 on an untested idea. However, I prefer to test with small classified ads first. By doing so, I can determine the product's sales appeal and potential for under $200.

Your ad should seek inquiries, not orders. All requests for information should be immediately fulfilled with a powerful direct-mail sales letter, circular, order form, and reply envelope.

What should all this cost? A successful classified ad will bring in inquiries at a cost of 25 cents to $1 per lead. A good sales package will convert 10 percent to 35 percent of these leads to sales. I have run classified ads that pulled up to 17 times their cost in product sales.

5. *Don't underestimate the importance of the bounce-back catalog.* A bounce-back catalog is a circular containing descriptions and order information for your complete line of related information products. When a customer orders your lead product, you insert the bounce-back catalog in the package and ship it with the order. Ideally, the customer sees the catalog, scans it, orders more items, and his or her order bounces back to you.

The bounce-back catalog doesn't have to be long or elaborate. For my mail order business, the catalog is printed on four 8½-by-11-inch pages in black ink on colored paper.

Additional sales generated by bounce-backs can range from 10 percent to 100 percent of the front-end sales generated by your original ad or mailing. The only cost is a few cents to print each catalog sheet. There is no postage cost, because the catalog gets a free ride as an insert in your product shipment. (*Tip:* When you fulfill a bounce-back order, send out another bounce-back catalog . . . and another . . . until the customer has bought every item in the catalog.)

6. *Create low-, medium-, and high-priced products.* Different buyers have different perceptions of what your information is worth and what they will pay. You will get more sales by testing a variety of prices for your lead item and by offering a number of different products reflecting a broad range of prices.

My front-end product is a $12 book. The back end consists of a series of $7 and $8 reports, a second book for $20, and a six-tape cassette album for $49.95. Dr. Jeffrey Lant, who sells business development products and services, has products ranging from a $4 report to a $4,800 consulting service.

Once I sent an inquiry to a well-known and successful marketer who specializes in selling information on how to make money as a speaker. But I didn't buy because the only alternatives were a large cassette album or a one-year newsletter subscription, both of which were fairly expensive, and I wasn't ready to make that kind of commitment to the subject. Most buyers prefer to sample your information with a lower-priced product, such as a book, single cassette, or inexpensive manual in the $10 to $50 range.

7. *Let your buyers tell you what products they want you to create.* Always put your name, address, and phone number in every information product you produce, and encourage feedback from readers. Many readers become advocates and fans, calling, writing, and establishing a dialogue with you.

Welcome this. Not only can you solve their problems and answer their inquiries by telling them which current products to buy, but their questions can suggest new products. *Most of my back-end products were created to answer specific questions readers asked me repeatedly.* Instead of having the same telephone conversation over and over again, I can simply sell them a report that contains the answers they seek. It saves time and generates revenue.

8. *Be the quality source.* Your strongest advertisement is a good product. A clever or deceptive ad can certainly generate brisk sales, and returns may not be excessive even if your product is poor, but customers will feel cheated and will not favor you with repeat business.

A good product will have people actively seeking you out and will bring in a small but steady stream of phone calls, letters, inquiries, and orders generated by the product itself and not the advertising. You will be shocked at the enormous effort some people expend to locate the source of quality information products that are well spoken of by other buyers.

USING SMALL ADS TO SELL INFORMATION PRODUCTS

The least expensive way to start in mail order is with small classified ads. Actually, these ads generate a greater return on investment than any other medium, including full-page ads. With a winning classified ad and strong inquiry fulfillment kit, you have the foundation for making your home-based information products business profitable.

You should not ask for an order directly from a classified ad. It won't work. There is not enough copy in a classified ad to make the complete sale.

Classified advertising is two-step direct marketing. In step one, you run a small classified ad to generate an inquiry, which is a request for a brochure or other information about your product. In step two, the prospect reads the literature you send, then orders the product.

The way to measure classified ad response for inquiry advertising is to divide the cost of the ad by the number of inquiries, and thus determine the cost per inquiry. For instance, if you run a classified ad and it costs you $100, and you get 50 inquiries, your cost per inquiry is $2.

When people inquire, you send them an inquiry fulfillment kit, which is a sales package promoting your product. The inquiry fulfillment kit consists of an outer envelope, sales letter, circular or brochure, order form, and reply envelope.

Bernard Lyons, editor of *KEY Newsletter*, says that classified ads must follow the AIDA principle, meaning they must get attention, generate interest, create desire for the product, and ask for action. According to Lyons, sales appeals that work in classified mail order advertising include promises of saving time, eliminating worry and fear, satisfying curiosity, avoiding work or risk, and obtaining love, money, health, popularity, leisure, security, entertainment, self-confidence, better appearance, prestige, pride of accomplishment, success, self-expression, pride of ownership, comfort, creativity, and self-improvement.

Lyons says the six most effective words and phrases to use in your classified ads are: free, new, amazing, now, how to, and easy. To this list I would add: discover, method, plan, reveals, show, simple, startling, advanced, improved, and you.

One of my most successful mail order ads, run continuously for many years in *Writer's Digest*, reads as follows:

MAKE $85,000/YEAR writing ads, brochures, promotional materials for local/national client. Free details: CTC, 22 E. Quackenbush, Dept. WD, Dumont, NJ 07628.

Here are some other examples of how to write classified mail order ads:

EXTRA CASH. 12 ways to make money at home. Free details. . . .

MAIL-ORDER MILLIONAIRE reveals money-making secrets.
FREE 1-hour cassette. . . .

SELL NEW BOOK by mail! 400% profit! Free dealer information. . . .

GROW earthworms at home for profit. . . .

CARNIVOROUS AND WOODLAND terrarium plants. Send for FREE catalog. . . .

ANCESTOR HUNTING? Trace your family roots the easy way. Details free. . . .

The way to generate the most response is to ask for an inquiry, not an order. This is done by putting a phrase such as "free details," "free information," or "free catalog," followed by a colon and your address.

Some mail order advertisers ask the prospect to pay for the information, either by sending a small amount of money (25 cents, 50 cents, $1, and $2 are typical) or by requiring the prospect to send a self-addressed stamped envelope.

The theory is that asking for postage or a nominal payment brings you a more qualified lead and therefore results in a higher percentage of leads converted to sales. My experience is that it doesn't pay to charge for your information kit, since doing so dramatically cuts down on the number of leads you will receive.

As a rule of thumb, whenever you offer information to generate an inquiry, make it free. The exception might be a very expensive and elaborate catalog, for which you charge $1 to cover your costs.

Key code all your promotions, so you can track which ad or mailing each inquiry or order comes from. In your classified ads, put the key code in the address. For instance, in my ad "MAKE $85,000/YEAR writing," the key code "WD" refers to *Writer's Digest* magazine. Since the ad runs every month, I don't bother adding a code number to track the month. If you wanted to do so, you could. For example, "Dept. WD-10" would mean *Writer's Digest* magazine, October issue (the tenth month of the year). Keep track of the key code on each inquiry and record the information using the form in Appendix C.

The measure of a successful inquiry classified ad is the cost per inquiry. Therefore, if you can get your message across in fewer words, you pay less for the ad and as a result lower your cost per inquiry.

Make your classifieds as short and pithy as possible. Here are some tips for reducing your word count:

- ✔ Be concise. Use the minimum number of words needed to communicate your idea. For example, instead of "Earn $500 a Day in Your Own Home-Based Business," write "Work at Home—$500/Day!"

- ✔ Minimize your address. You pay the publication for every word in your classified, including your address. Therefore, instead of "22 E. Quackenbush Avenue," I write "22 E. Quackenbush." The mail still gets delivered, and I save one word. This can add up to significant savings for ads run frequently in multiple publications.

- ✔ Use phrases and sentence fragments rather than full sentences.

- ✔ Remember your objective. You are looking for only an inquiry, not an order. You don't need a lot of copy, since all you are asking the reader to do is send for free information.

- ✔ Use combination words, hyphenated words, and slash constructions. For instance, instead of "Grow earth worms," which is three words, write "Grow earthworms," which counts as two words, saving you a word.

Place your classified ads in publications that run mail-order classified ad sections. Send for free media kits, which include details on circulation, advertising rates, readership, and a sample issue of the publication. Ask for several issues, if the publisher will send them.

Look at the classified ad sections in the publications. Are their ads for products similar to yours? This is a good sign. See if these ads repeat from issue to issue. The advertisers would not repeat them unless they were working. If this publication is working for their offers, it can work for yours, too.

Classified ad sections are divided by various headings. Place your ad in the appropriate section. If you don't see an appropriate heading, call the magazine and ask if it will create one for you.

If you sell information by mail, avoid putting your classified under the heading "Books and Booklets." This will reduce orders. Instead, put the ad under a heading related to the subject matter. For example, if you are selling a book on how to make money cleaning chimneys, place the ad under "Business Opportunities."

We have already mentioned the two key measurements of two-step classified advertising, which are the cost per inquiry and the percentage of inquiries converted to orders.

The bottom line is whether the sales the ad generated exceeded the cost of the ad space. If they did, it was profitable. If they didn't, the ad isn't working and a new ad should be tested.

Appendix C contains a form you can use to track inquiries and sales from your classified ads. Once the sheet is completed, you can, at a glance, compare the cost of the ad space with the total sales generated. My goal is to generate sales at least twice what the ad space costs. Your objectives may be different.

You can test a classified by running it just one time in a publication. The problem is, most magazines and even weekly newspapers have long lead times—several weeks or more—for placing classified ads. If you place the ad to run one time only, and the ad pulls well, you then have to wait several weeks or months until you can get it in again.

In a weekly newspaper or magazine, I test a classified ad by running it for one month—four consecutive issues. For a monthly publication, I test it for three months—three consecutive issues. If the first insertion is profitable, I will probably extend the insertion order for several months, so the ad runs continuously with no interruption.

With a full-page ad, you usually get the greatest number of orders the first time the ad runs in the magazine. Response declines with each additional insertion, and at the point where the ad is not going to be profitable in its next insertion, you pull it and try another ad.

The reason is that the first time the ad runs, it skims the cream of the prospects, getting orders from those most likely to buy. Obviously, those who buy from the first insertion of the ad will not buy when it runs again. Therefore, each time the ad runs, it reaches a smaller and smaller audience of potential new buyers.

With a classified ad, however, the total response is much less for each insertion. Therefore, it doesn't materially affect the number of po-

A classified ad will generate a greater return compared to its insertion cost than any other size ad. However, the total sales are naturally modest. If you want to make more sales faster, use full-page display ads.

tential first-time customers the ad appeals to. In fact, some people who responded once, got your sales literature, and didn't buy, may respond several times—and get your literature several times—before they eventually break down and buy. Also, each issue reaches a number of new subscribers via subscriptions and newsstand circulation, so the total audience of potential new buyers for a classified remains fairly constant in number.

While response to full-page mail order ads declines with each insertion, the response to a classified ad can remain steady for many insertions. Indeed, some information marketers (and I am one of them) have run the same classified monthly in the same magazine for years at a time, with no decline in response. In fact, response sometimes tends to increase during the first 12 months the ad is run, as people see the ad over and over again, and eventually become curious enough to respond.

Increasing Your Income Through Consulting

While most professional speakers prefer to speak to groups, some clients want your advice as one-on-one consulting. You can bill anywhere from $50 to $500 an hour, or $400 to $4,000 a day, giving such consulting advice on a per diem or per contract basis.

What does it take to be a consultant? "A strong stomach," replies management consultant Gary Blake. Self-employment offers a potential for greater financial rewards and self-fulfillment than working for someone else, but there is also greater risk and uncertainty.

In the book *Setting Up Shop: The Do's and Don'ts of Starting a Small Business* (McGraw-Hill), Randy Baca Smith discusses the personality traits shared by most entrepreneurial people. Smith's ideal entrepreneur is: a self-starter, a people person, a leader, a good organizer, a hard worker, trustworthy, responsible, decisive, energetic, and in good health.

For consultants, I'd add a few more items to the list:

- ✔ The consultant has to be part loner, part extrovert. As a consultant, you'll spend 90 percent of your time working alone. But you must be enthusiastic and outgoing in your meetings with prospects and clients.

- ✔ Consultants must be good salespeople. Unlike corporate employees, whose supervisors set the assignments, the consultant must land a contract for each job. If the idea of going out and selling yourself makes you uneasy, consulting is not for you.

✔ Consultants enjoy their work and are exceptionally good at it.

✔ Consultants despise hierarchies, long chains of command, rigid thinking, inaction, and set routines.

✔ They embrace new problems and projects, unconventional approaches, and unstructured environments.

✔ They're curious, creative, self-confident, and optimistic.

WHAT ARE THE ADVANTAGES AND DRAWBACKS OF CONSULTING?

Consulting has many advantages: independence, autonomy, variety, money, the opportunity to set your own goals and pursue your own interests, and the status of being recognized as an expert in your field.

Naturally, there are negatives as well as positives. Separated from the corporation, you might miss the prestige, the power, and the sense of belonging you had as a communications manager. You'll give up the benefits, the expense account, the annual office Christmas party, and, worst of all, the steady paycheck.

Draw up your own list of personal pros and cons, and see whether you're still tempted to set up your own shop.

John, a 27-year-old advertising manager, was bored supervising his company's advertising program. He wanted to start his own communications consulting firm, but few companies hire freelance advertising managers. How could he develop a salable specialty?

John had spent six months establishing an in-house system for fulfilling, qualifying, and tracking sales leads. He had even written an article about the experience for an advertising journal. Realizing that thousands of industrial-business marketers need help handling leads, John quit his job to start a consulting firm specializing in inquiry fulfillment systems. Using a one-page sales letter mailed with reprints of his article, John landed his first major contract within six weeks.

If you're a manager or an administrator, focus on a single skill or area and become an expert in it. Some of today's most in-demand consulting specialties include e-business, information technology, technical writing, business writing, data communications, software development, direct marketing, active listening, negotiating, speaking, and presentation skills.

Take a look at what companies need. In what areas do they use high-paid consultants or freelancers? Those are the specialties you want to break into. The best source of prospects for your consulting practice is companies that hire you to give seminars or workshops, then decide they want more customized help. Another good source of leads is people in the audience at your public seminars and association speeches. Also, don't neglect people you already know: coworkers, colleagues, suppliers, acquaintances, business contacts, friends, even relatives.

Advertising and promotion can generate dozens of new leads. Direct mail is particularly effective for reaching selected audiences such as human resources managers, training directors, CEOs, or sales managers. And the cost of direct mail is controllable since you can mail as few or as many pieces as you wish. Always include a business reply postcard or other response element with your mailing to increase its pull.

Space advertising is usually not cost-effective for independent consultants. But I've run small classified ads in specialty publications, and they've paid for themselves many times over.

HOW DO I MAKE A FIRST SALE?

- ✔ Give a free consultation. Since you don't have a track record, you have to prove yourself. A free demonstration of your skills and services lets prospects evaluate you firsthand. One ad agency I know of offers to provide prospective clients with a free evaluation of their current advertising programs. To be an effective sales tool, the free consultation must give useful advice to the prospect, demonstrate why he or she should hire you, and take a minimum amount of time.

- ✔ Work "on spec." A variation of the free consultation is to do work on speculation (on spec). This means the client doesn't pay unless satisfied with your work. Many ad agencies prepare on-spec preliminary campaigns when they pursue new accounts.

- ✔ Charge less than the competition. As a novice consultant, you may have to do more work for less pay to make your first sale. After you make your first few sales, you can charge new clients more competitive rates.

HOW DO I SET MY FEES?

In a "Peanuts" cartoon strip, Charlie Brown asks Lucy why she charges a mere five cents for a session at her sidewalk psychiatry stand. Lucy's reply: "It's what the market will bear."

Your fee will be determined by the going rates for your type of service as well as by the demand for you in particular. Self-confidence also plays a part; often you can command a higher fee just by asking for it. Of course, I assume you want to be fair to both yourself and your clients.

In every consulting specialty, there's a broad but definite range of what consultants charge. Just as an attorney charges a higher hourly rate than a gardener or a handyman, a management consultant's fees are higher than those of a mechanical artist.

While you still have your job, contact half a dozen consultants in your field and ask what they're charging. Their answers will guide you in establishing your own fee schedule.

Most consultants charge either by the day (per diem), by the hour, by a monthly retainer, or by the project. Set fees based on the best estimate of how long a project will take to complete.

When you get an assignment, get it in writing. A purchase order or letter of authorization clarifies the scope of the project and helps avoid misunderstandings later on. The purchase order should state the type of project, fee, deadline, and charges for revisions, if any. For first-time clients, especially smaller firms, consider collecting all or part of your fee in advance.

Jaws drop when consultants mention their $200-an-hour or $2,000-a-day rates. But remember, those fees apply to billable time—time spent working on consulting projects. The consultant's income is zero dollars an hour during the hours spent marketing and running the business, as well as during vacations, coffee breaks, and lunch. "The economics of freelance writing are very simple," writes *Advertising Age* columnist James Brady. "No write, no pay." The same holds true for consulting.

WHERE DO I GO FROM HERE?

In corporate life, career paths are clearly mapped out. At the ad agency, for example, the junior copywriters become senior copywriters; the senior copywriters become creative directors; the creative directors become vice presidents; and the vice presidents become senior vice presidents.

The consultant's career path is less well defined; if you're self-employed, you can't covet the boss's position. As a result, your goals become achievements rather than job titles.

A consultant I know has the goal of winning new accounts in three different high-tech areas: telecommunications, microcomputers, and electronic publishing. Another wants to be the leading expert in his field, direct mail copywriting, and has hired a press agent to help accomplish this.

People are silently begging to be led. They are crying out to know more about your product or service. When you educate your customers, you'll see your profits soar. Educate your prospective buyers about everything (including a few of the bad or less positive aspects of your product or service) and you'll sell to almost twice as many people as you do now.

—Jay Abraham, *Stealth Marketing* (Abraham Publishing Group)

A third wants his graphic arts studio to earn a quarter of its income from annual report work within two years.

Becoming an authority, taking on challenging assignments, making more money, working for prestigious clients—these are some of the things consultants strive for.

Think about what you would like to do. Do you want to write a book on your consulting and speaking specialty, earn $1,000 a day, or become a popular lecturer?

Identify your career goals, and commit them to paper. With a well-defined plan guiding your communications consulting firm, a consulting career can provide a lifetime of fun, challenge, and financial reward—not to mention the satisfaction of being your own boss.

Appendix A

Bibliography

BOOKS

Bermont, Hubert, *How to Become a Successful Consultant in Your Own Field* (Prima Publishing, 1995).

Bly, Robert, *The Copywriter's Handbook: A Step-by-Step Guide to Writing Copy That Sells* (New York: Henry Holt & Co., 1990). How to write effective copy.

———, *Getting Your Book Published* (Yonkers, NY: Roblin Press, 1997). How to get a nonfiction book published. Includes sample book proposal, lists of agents and publishers, and more.

———, *The Perfect Sales Piece* (New York: John Wiley & Sons, 1993). Guide to creating effective brochures, catalogs, and other sales literature.

———, *Power-Packed Direct Mail* (New York: Henry Holt & Co., 1995). A guide to planning, writing, designing, and producing direct mail promotions.

———, *Selling Your Services* (New York: Henry Holt & Co., 1994). Selling skills for service providers.

———, *Targeted Public Relations* (New York: Henry Holt & Co., 1996). A handbook on how to do public relations.

Caples, John, *Tested Advertising Methods* (Englewood Cliffs, NJ: Prentice Hall, 1974). Secrets of writing effective space ads.

Cates, Bill, *Unlimited Referrals* (Wheaton, MD: Thunder Hill Press, 1996). How to get lots of referral leads.

Cohen, William, *How to Make It Big as a Consultant* (New York: AMA-COM, 1993).

Floyd, Elaine, *Marketing with Newsletters* (St. Louis, MO: Newsletter Resources, 1994). How to create effective promotional newsletters.

Garratt, Sally, *Going It Alone: How to Survive and Thrive as an Independent Consultant* (Goward Publishing, 1994).

Harris, Godfrey, with J. Harris, *Generate Word of Mouth Advertising: 101 Easy and Inexpensive Ways to Promote Your Business* (Los Angeles, CA: The Americas Group, 1995). Interesting, innovative low-cost promotions for yourself and your clients.

Holtz, Herman, *The Complete Guide to Being an Independent Contractor* (Dearborn, 1995).

————, *How to Succeed as an Independent Consultant* (New York: John Wiley & Sons, 1993).

————, *Proven Proposal Strategies to Win More Business* (Dearborn, 1997).

Lant, Jeffrey, *E-Mail Eldorado* (Cambridge, MA: JLA Publications, 1994). Best book I've seen on generating leads and sales using direct mail on the Internet.

————, *No More Cold Calls* (Cambridge, MA: JLA Publications, 1994). How to generate leads for your service business.

Muldoon, Katie, *How to Profit through Catalog Marketing* (Lincolnwood, IL: NTC Business Books, 1996). Recommended for anyone writing catalog copy.

Ogilvy, David, *Ogilvy on Advertising* (New York: Crown, 1989). Required for every copywriter writing print ads.

Osgood, Charles, *Osgood on Speaking* (New York: William Morrow, 1988). Brief, solid, easy-to-read how-to book on giving a talk.

Parker, Roger C., *Roger C. Parker's Guide to Web Content and Design* (New York: MIS Press, 1997). Best book I've ever seen on creating effective Web sites.

Reeves, Rosser, *Reality in Advertising* (New York: Alfred A. Knopf, 1985). Excellent book on how to increase advertising effectiveness.

Rosenberg, Paul, *How to Be a Successful Computer Consultant* (Englewood Cliffs, NJ: Prentice Hall, 1995).

Ruhl, Janet, *The Computer Consultant's Guide: Real-Life Strategies for Building a Successful Consulting Career* (New York: John Wiley & Sons, 1994).

Shenson, Howard, *Shenson on Consulting* (New York: John Wiley & Sons, 1990).

Simon, Alan R., *How to Be a Successful Computer Consultant* (New York: McGraw-Hill Computer Books, 1993).

Smith, Terry, *Making Successful Presentations* (New York: John Wiley &

Sons, 1984). Excellent guide to writing and delivering workplace, instructional, and sales and marketing presentations.

Stone, Bob, *Successful Direct Marketing Methods* (Chicago, IL: NTC Business Books). Everything you need to know about direct marketing.

Tepper, Ron, *Become a Top Consultant* (New York: John Wiley & Sons, 1987).

Tuller, Lawrence, *Cutting Edge Consultants* (New York: Simon & Schuster, 1992).

Vitale, Joe, *CyberWriting: How to Promote Your Product or Service Online* (New York: AMACOM, 1997). How to write copy for the Internet.

Walters, Dottie, and Lilly Walters, *Speak and Grow Rich* (Englewood Cliffs, NJ: Prentice Hall, 1989). How to make money as a professional speaker.

PERIODICALS

Advertising Age
740 North Rush Street
Chicago, IL 60611
312-649-5200

Adweek Magazine
49 East 21st Street
New York, NY 10010
212-529-5500

The Art of Self Promotion
P.O. Box 23
Hoboken, NJ 07030
201-653-0783

Burt Dubin Private Letter
1 Speaking Success Road
Kingman, AZ 86402-6543
502-753-7531

Business Marketing
740 North Rush Street
Chicago, IL 60611
312-649-5260

Commerce Business Daily
Government Printing Office
Washington, DC
202-512-0000

Computer Consultants &
*   Contractors Newsletter*
Corry Publishing
2840 West 21st Street
Erie, PA 16506
814-838-0025

The Consultant's Craft
Summit Consulting Group
Box 1009
East Greenwich, RI 02818
800-766-7935

Contract Professional
125 Walnut Street
Watertown, MA 02172
617-926-5818

Direct Marketing Magazine
Hoke Communications
224 Seventh Street
Garden City, NY 11530
516-746-6700

DM NEWS
Mill Hollow
19 West 21st Street
New York, NY 10010
212-741-2095

Executive Speechwriter Newsletter
Emerson Falls Business Park
St. Johnsbury, VT 05819
802-748-4472

Industrial Marketing Practitioner
1661 Valley Forge Road, #245
Lansdale, PA 19446
215-362-7200

Journal of Management Consulting
858 Longview Road
Burlingame, CA 94010
650-342-1954

Priorities
Franklin Covey Co.
2200 West Parkway Boulevard
Salt Lake City, UT 84119
800-767-1776

Public Relations Journal
33 Irving Place
New York, NY 10003
212-998-2230

Sales and Marketing Management
633 Third Avenue
New York, NY 10017
212-986-4800

Sharing Ideas
P.O. Box 1120
Glendora, CA 92711
626-335-8069

Successful Meetings
Bill Publications
633 Third Avenue
New York, NY 10017
212-592-6200

The Successful Practice
Media Publishers, Inc.
2085 Commercial Street NE
Salem, OR 97303
503-371-1390

Target Marketing Magazine
North American Publishing Co.
401 N. Broad Street
Philadelphia, PA 19108
215-238-5300

Training Magazine
50 South Ninth Street
Minneapolis, MN 55402
612 333-0471

Training & Development
1640 King Street
Alexandria, VA 22314
703-683-8100

DIRECTORIES

Bacon's Publicity Checklist
332 South Michigan Avenue
Chicago, IL 60604
800-621-0561

Media lists for mailing press releases.

Directory of Corporate Meeting Planners
Directory of Association Meeting Planners & Conference/ Convention Directors
Macmillan Directory Division
1140 Broadway
New York, NY 10001
800-223-1797

Directory of Top Computer Executives
Applied Computer Research
Box 92277
Phoenix, AZ 85071-2266
800-234-2227

Good prospecting directory for computer consultants.

The Encyclopedia of Associations
Gale Research
Book Tower
Detroit, MI 48226
313-961-2242

Associations to whose membership lists you can target promotions.

The Interactive Multimedia Sourcebook
R. R. Bowker
121 Chanlon Road
New Providence, NJ 07974
908-464-6800

Sourcebook for marketers interested in Internet promotion.

National Directory of Mailing Lists
Oxbridge Communications
150 Fifth Avenue
New York, NY 10114-0235
800-955-0231

Directory containing descriptions and contact information for 15,000 mailing lists.

O'Dwyer's Directory of Corporate Communications
J.R. O'Dwyer Company, Inc.
271 Madison Avenue
New York, NY 10016
212-679-2471

Directory of public relations firms.

Standard Directory of Advertisers
R. R. Bowker
121 Chanlon Road
New Providence, NJ 07974
908-464-6800

Directory of advertising agencies.

Standard Rate and Data Service
1700 Higgins Road
Des Plaines, IL 60018-5605
847-375-5000
Comprehensive directory of
publications that accept advertising.

Appendix

Software

BUSINESS PLANNING

Business Plan Pro
Palo Alto Software
800-229-7526

MasterPlan Professional
MAUS Business Systems
509-663-9523

BuzPlan Builder Interactive
Jian Co.
800-440-5426

Plan Write
Business Resource Software
800-423-1228

LEAD TRACKING AND CONTACT MANAGEMENT

Act
Symantech
800-441-7234

LPS
Simplified Office Systems
16025 Van Aken Boulevard
Suite 102
Cleveland, OH 44120
216-572-1050

FastTrack
Fastech and Gelco Information
    Network
400 Parkway Drive
Broomall, PA 19008
610-359-9200

MailEasy
Applied Information Group
720 King Georges Road
Fords, NJ 08863
908-738-8444

GoldMine
GoldMine Software
800-654-3526

Mail Order Manager (MOM)
Dydacomp Development
  Corporation
150 River Road, Suite N-1
Montville, NJ 07045
201-335-1256

Marketing Professional's
  InfoCenter/Smart Marketing
  Suite
Group One Software
4200 Parliament Place, Suite 600
Lanham, MD 20706
301-918-0721

Maximizer 97is
Maximizer Technologies
800-804-6299

MSM
Marketing Information Services
1840 Oak Avenue
Suite 400
Evanston, IL 60201
847-491-0682

Order Power!
Computer Solutions, Inc.
6187 NW 167th Street, Unit H33
Miami, FL 33015
305-558-7000

Postalsoft
439 Mormon Coulsee Road
LaCross, WI 54601
608-788-8700

Pro-Mail
Software Marketing Associates
2080 Silas Deane Highway
Rocky Hill, CT 06067-2341
860-721-8929

Profit Smart
Digital Arts LLC
1551 Valley Forge Road, Suite 259
Lansdale, PA 19446-5459
215-361-2650

Telemagic
800-835-MAGIC

Appendix C

Forms

FORM FOR RECORDING DATA ON SALES LEADS

Date _____ Source of inquiry _____ Response via _____
Name_____ Title _____
Company _____ Phone _____
Address _____ Room/floor _____
City _____ State _____ Zip _____
Type of business:_____
Type of accounts (if an ad agency):_____
Type of projects:_____
For: ❑ Immediate project ❑ Future reference
Project to be started in: _____
(month/year)
STATUS:
❑ Sent package on (date): _____
❑ Enclosed these samples: _____
❑ Next step is to: _____
❑ Probability of assignment:_____
❑ Comments: _____
_____
_____

Contact Record:
Date: _____ Summary:_____
_____

FORM FOR TRACKING AD RESPONSE

Month _____ Year _____

Ad or mailing _____ Key code _____

Product_____ Offer _____

Total cost _____ Total sales _____

Day	# Inquiries	Total Inquiries to date	Day's Sales	Total Sales to date
1				
2				
3				
4				
5				
6				
7				
8				
9				
10				
11				
12				
13				
14				
15				
16				
17				
18				
19				
20				
21				
22				
23				
24				
25				
26				
27				
28				
29				
30				
31				

INSERTION ORDER

Use this insertion order form to place lead-generating classified and space ads in appropriate media. By establishing yourself as an "agency," you will often be granted the 15 percent ad agency commission. This saves you 15 percent on the cost of the ad space. When copying the form, insert your own company name and address at the top.

Advertising Insertion Order

From:

ABC Ad Agency
123 Main Street
Anytown, USA
Phone: 123-555-1234

Date:

Advertiser:

Product:

To:

Publication in which ad is to run:_____

Date of insertion:_____

Size of ad:_____

Instructions:

Rate:_____

Less frequency discount _____%

Less agency commission_____% on gross

Less cash discount _____% on net

Net amount on this insertion order:_____

Insertion order placed by:_____

TELEMARKETING CALL SHEETS

Date _____ Telemarketer Name _____

ABC Consulting Company
Prospect Data Sheet

Name _____
Title _____
Company _____
Street Address _____
City, State, Zip _____
Phone_____
Fax _____
E-mail_____

Call Attempts

Date _____ Time _____   Date_____ Time _____
Date _____ Time _____   Date_____ Time _____

Contact

❑ Prospect busy. Call back on_____ At_____ (Day, Time)
    Best time to call _____ (time of day)
❑ Long-term call back during_____ of_____ (month, year)
❑ Phone presentation made on _____ (month, day, year)
❑ Left message to return call

Action

❑ Appointment set for_____ at_____ (month, day, time)
❑ Referral given:

    _____
    _____

❑ Not interested. Reason:

    _____
    _____

Current Company Information:

Number of employees: _____
Types of services needed: _____

Date_____ Telemarketer Name_____

ABC Consulting Company
Daily Activity Sheet

Outbound Calls

Number of:

Dials _____

Busy signals _____

Voice mail messages _____

Call backs scheduled _____

Presentations _____

Literature sent _____

Appts booked _____

No interest _____

Referrals given _____

Inbound Calls

Number of:

Query calls _____

Presentations _____

Literature sent _____

Appointments booked _____

Organizations and Public Seminar Companies

ORGANIZATIONS

American Association for Adult
and Continuing Education
1112 16th Street NW
Suite 420
Washington, DC 20036
202-463-6333

American Consultants League
1290 Palm Avenue
Sarasota, FL 34236
813-952-9290

American Seminar Leaders
Association
101 Providence Mine Road
Suite 105
Nevada City, CA 95959
800-735-0511

Premiere association for
professional seminar leaders.

American Society for Training and
Development
1640 King Street
Alexandria, VA 22314
703-683-8100

Largest society for corporate
training professionals.

American Society of Association
Executives
1575 I Street NW
Washington, DC 20005
202-626-ASAE

Business Marketing Association
150 North Wacker Drive
Suite 1760
Chicago, IL 60606
312-409-4262

Business to Business Direct
  Marketing Conference
Box 4232
Stamford, CT 06907-0232
203-358-9900

The Consultants Bureau
P.O. Box 10057
New Brunswick, NJ 08906-0057
908-747-5786

Consultants National Resource
  Center
27-A Big Spring Road, P.O. Box 430
Clear Spring, MD 21722
301-791-9332

Consultants' Network
57 West 89th Street
New York, NY 10024
212-799-5239

Dale Carnegie
780 Third Avenue
New York, NY 10017
800-231-5800
Web site: www.dalecarnegie.com

Direct Marketing Association
1120 Avenue of the Americas
New York, NY 10036-6700
212-768-7277

Direct Marketing to Business
Target Conference Corporation
90 Grove Street
Ridgefield, CT 06877
203-438-6602

Independent Computer
  Consultants Association
933 Gardenview Office Parkway
St. Louis, MO 63141
900-774-4222

Institute of Management
  Consultants
521 Fifth Avenue, 35th Floor
New York, NY 10175-3598
212-697-8262

International Group of Agents
  and Bureaus
18825 Hicrest Road
P.O. Box 1120
Glendora, CA 91740
800-438-1242
Web site: www.igab.org

Association of speakers bureaus
and lecture agents.

Langevin Learning Services
P.O. Box 1221
Ogdensburg, NY 13669-6221
800-223-2209
Web site: www.langevin.com

Training workshops for
professional trainers.

Learning Resources Network
1554 Hayes Drive
Manhattan, KS 66502
913-539-5376

Meeting Planners International
1950 Stemmons Freeway
Dallas, TX 75207
214-746-5248

National Association of Business
   Consultants
175 Fifth Avenue #2158
New York, NY 10010
800-571-6222

National Association of Computer
   Consultant Businesses
1250 Connecticut Avenue NW
Suite 700
Washington, DC 20036
202-637-6483

National Association of
   Management Consultants
4200 Wisconsin Avenue NW, #106
Washington, DC 20016
202-466-1601

National Speakers Association
1500 South Priest Drive
Tempe, AZ 85281
602-968-2552
Web site: www.nsaspeak.org

Largest association for professional
and aspiring speakers.

National Trade and Professional
   Association of America
1212 New York Avenue NW
Suite 330
Washington, DC 20005
202-898-0662

National University Continuing
   Education Association
One Dupont Plaza Circle, Suite 420
Washington, DC 20036
202-659-3130

Personal Achievement Institute
1 Speaking Success Road
Kingman, AZ 86402-6543
520-753-7546

"Speaking Success System," a
comprehensive information service
on how to make money as a
professional speaker.

Professional and Technical
   Consultants Association
P.O. Box 4143
Mountain View, CA 94040
800-286-8703

The Speaker's Platform
P.O. Box 21631
Santa Barbara, CA 93121
877-717-LEARN (5237), or
805-892-2386
Web site: www.speaking.com

For-profit Web site of speakers and
a speakers bureau.

Toastmasters International
P.O. Box 9052
Mission Viejo, CA 92609
714-858-8255

Walters International Speakers
   Bureau
P.O. Box 1120
Glendora, CA 91740
818-335-8069

Speakers bureau and publications
and workshops for speakers.

PUBLIC SEMINAR COMPANIES

These companies are in the business of public seminars. They put on many sessions and are often looking for presenters.

American Management Association
135 W. 50th Street
New York, NY 10020
212-903-7915

CareerTrack
3085 Center Green Drive
Boulder, CO 80301-5408
303-447-2323

Conference Board
845 Third Avenue
New York, NY 10022
212-759-0900

Dun & Bradstreet Corporation
    Foundation
Business Education Service
P.O. Box 3734
New York, NY 10008-3734
212-312-6880

Learning Dynamics, Inc.
29 Lansing Road
West Newton, MA 02165
617-332-7070

Learning International
225 High Ridge Road
Stamford, CT 06905
203-965-8400

Padgett Thompson of American
    Management Association
11221 Row Avenue
Leawood, KS 66211
800-255-4141

Performance Seminar Group
325 Myrtle Avenue
Bridgeport, CT 06604
203-366-2490, 800-222-2921

Pryor Resources, Inc.
2000 Shawnee Mission Parkway
Shawnee Mission, KS 66208
913-722-3990

Appendix E

Recommended Vendors

To accomplish some of the tasks outlined in this book, you may want to work with outside vendors. This list is by no means comprehensive—it simply lists the vendors I recommend in each category right now. A recommendation doesn't guarantee your satisfaction, so you should check out vendors thoroughly before hiring them. (This list is periodically updated on my Web site, www.bly.com.)

AUDIO AND VIDEO DUPLICATING

Cine Magnetics
100 Business Park Drive
Armonk, NY 10504-1750
800-431-1102 or 914-273-7500

AUDIOTAPING

Anthony Cioffi
Boulevard Productions
280 Boulevard
New Milford, NJ 07646
201-262-5202
Fax: 201-262-5216

BUSINESS PLANS

Lisa Hines
Business Plan Concepts
134 Oklyn Terrace
Lawrenceville, NJ 08648
609-530-0719

CARTOONS

The Cartoon Bank
A division of *New Yorker* Magazine
382 Warburton Avenue
Hastings on Hudson, NY 10706
800-897-8666, 914-478-5527
Web site: www.cartoonbank.com

Ted Goff
P.O. Box 22679
Kansas City, MO 64113
816-822-7370
Web site: www.tedgoff.com
E-mail: tgoff@tedgoff.com

CD-ROM DUPLICATION AND PACKAGING

Disc Makers
7905 North Route 130
Pennsauken, NJ 08110
800-237-6666

COMPETITIVE INTELLIGENCE

Brian Donnelly
Data Source International
200 Business Park Drive #304
Armonk, NY 10504
914-273-6100

Doug House
Washington Information Group
1350 Connecticut Avenue NW
#502
Washington, DC 20036
202-463-3284

DENTAL MARKETING

Dr. Travis McFee
1251 Lancaster Drive NE #B
Salem, OR 97301
503-587-9633

DIGITAL BUSINESS CARDS

Markus Schneider
Ember Media Corporation
1 World Trade Center, Suite 7967
New York, NY 10048
212-432-0040

DIGITAL PRINTING

Paul Lukas, Account Executive
Regent Group
20 West 20th Street
New York, NY 10011
212-691-9791

DIRECT MAIL GRAPHIC DESIGN

Lucien Cohen
1201 Broadway, #403
New York, NY 10001
212-685-7455

Lou Spina
225 West 36th Street, 5th Floor,
Room 2
New York, NY 10018
212-594-8955 (phone and fax)

Ray Holland
Holland Design
1450 Washington Boulevard
Stamford, CT 06902
203-329-6633
Fax: 203-329-7954

Ms. Elaine Tannenbaum
Elaine Tannenbaum Design
310 West 106th Street, Apt. 16D
New York, NY 10025
212-769-2096
Fax: 212-712-1990

Bob McCarron
M/Comm Creative Resources
15 East 12th Street, 2d Floor
New York, NY 10003
212-645-7554

Karen Weinstein
16 Stuyvesant Oval, 12F
New York, NY 10009
212-533-0103

DIRECT MAIL MONITORING

Advanced Monitor Systems
75 Lake Road, Suite 370
Congers, NY 10920-2323
914-639-7656

U.S. Monitoring Service
86 Maple Avenue
New City, NY 10956-5036
800-767-7967, 914-634-1331

DIRECT MAIL PRINTERS

KoBel Inc.
115 Catamount Drive, #102
Milton, VT 05468
800-893-6000

DIRECT MARKETING ATTORNEYS

John Awerdick
Williams, Caliri, Miller & Ottley
1428 Route 23
Wayne, NJ 07474
973-694-3695

Linda Goldstein
Hall, Dickler, Kent, Friedman &
    Wood
909 Third Avenue
New York, NY 10022
212-339-5400

E-BUSINESS

Bob Bly
22 East Quackenbush Avenue
Dumont, NJ 07628
201-385-1220
Fax: 201-385-1138
email: rwbly@bly.com
Web site: www.bly.com

Susan Mintzer
Quadrix
255 Old New Brunswick Road
Suite South 220
Piscataway, NJ 08854
732-235-2600
E-commerce Web sites.

Michelle Feit
e-Post Direct
1 Blue Hill Plaza
Pearl River, NY 10965
800-409-4443
Fax: 914-620-9035
Web site: www.epostdirect.com
E-mail: michelle.feit@edithroman.com

FAX MARKETING

Business Link International
90 Douglas Pike
Smithfield, RI 02197
800-929-1643

Maury S. Kauffman
The Kauffman Group
324 Windsor Drive
Cherry Hill, NJ 08002-2426
609-482-8288

Sarah East Stambler
Marketing with Technology
370 Central Park West, #210
New York, NY 10025-6517
212-222-1713

FOCUS GROUPS

Donald G. Heilala
Industrial Research Center
628 Brooke Lane, Suite 201
Glen Mills, PA 19342
610-459-4707

GRAPHIC DESIGN, BROCHURES

Mr. Steve Brown
Brown & Company
138 Joralemon Street #4R
Brooklyn, NY 11201
718-875-0674
E-mail: browncompany
   @yahoo.com
E-mail: pubart@yahoo.com

Leslie Nolan
Nolan Design
1211 Sixteenth Avenue
Belmar, NJ 07718
732-280-7989
Fax: 732-280-7998

Paul Spadafora
Park Ridge Marketing
1776 On The Green
67 Park Place
Morristown, NJ 07960
201-984-2622

HIGH-IMPACT DIRECT MAIL (EXPRESS MAILINGS)

Response Mail Express
4517 George Road, #200
Tampa, FL 33634
813-243-1938

ILLUSTRATION

Bob Calleja
490 Elm Avenue
Bogota, NJ 07603
201-488-3028
Fax: 201-488-3527

David McCoy
28 Hilltop Terrace
Bloomingdale, NJ 07403
973-283-4323
e-mail: davetoons@aol.com

INFOMERCIALS

Andrew Cohen
DRI
New York, NY
212-226-0060

Scott Wooley
Five Star
Boca Raton, FL
561-279-7827

Karen Geller
ADM
40 Seaview Boulevard
Port Washington, NY 11050
800-ADM-DIAL, 516-484-6900

LETTER SHOP

Steve Grech
Dispatch Letter Service
New York, NY
212-307-5943

Mr. Jerry Lake
Jerry Lake Mailing Service
Airport Industrial Park
620 Frelinghuysen Avenue
Newark, NJ 07114
973-565-9268

Mitch Hisiger
Fala Direct Marketing
70 Marcus Drive
Melville, NY 11747
516-694-1919

LIBRARY RESEARCH

Bob Concoby
1675 East Main, #221
Kent, OH 44240
330-498-0921
Fax: 330-966-8055
E-mail: concoby@usa.net

Mr. John Maddux
2665 Leda Court
Cincinnati, OH 45211
513-662-9176

LITERARY AGENTS

Bob Diforio
D4EO Literary Agency
7 Indian Valley Road
Weston, CT 06883
203-544-7180
Fax: 203-544-7160 fax
E-mail: d4eo@home.com

Faith Hamlin
Sanford J. Greenburger
   Associates Inc.
55 Fifth Avenue, 15th Floor
New York, NY 10003
212-206-5607

B. K. Nelson
84 Woodland
Pleasantville, NY 10570
914-741-1323

Tony Seidl
TD Media
300 East 59th Street #1706
New York, NY 10022
212-588-0807

Scott Waxman
Scott Waxman Agency
1650 Broadway #1101
New York, NY 10019
212-262-2388

MAILINGS LISTS

Direct Media
200 Pemberwick Road
Greenwich, CT 06830
203-532-1000

Mr. Ken Morris
Morris Direct Marketing
300 West 55th Street #19D
New York, NY 10019
212-757-7711

Mr. Steve Roberts
Edith Roman Associates
P.O. Box 1556
Pearl River, NY 10965
800-223-2194

MARKET RESEARCH

Terrence J. Pranses
Pranses Research Services
730 Park Avenue
Hoboken, NJ 07030-4006
201-659-2475

Peter Fondulas
Taylor Research & Consulting
6 Glenville Street
Greenwich, CT 06831
203-532-0202

MEDIA BUYING

David Geller & Associates
535 Fifth Avenue, 2d Floor
New York, NY 10017
212-455-0100

Linick Media
7 Putter Lane
Middle Island, NY 11953
516-924-8555

Maryanne Marillo
Manhattan Media
535 Fifth Avenue, 10th Floor
New York, NY 10017
212-807-4077

National Mail Order Advertising
P.O. Box 5
Sarasota, FL 34230
941-366-3003
E-mail: nmoc@gte.net

Novus Marketing
601 Lakeshore Parkway, #900
Minneapolis, MN 55305
612-476-7700

ON-HOLD ADVERTISING MESSAGES

Fred Guarino
Tikki
186 Glen Cove Avenue
Glen Cove, NY 11542
516-671-4555

On-Hold Marketing &
  Communications
4910 Urvandale Avenue
Des Moines, IA 51310
800-259-2769

PHOTOGRAPHERS

Jonathan Clymer
Jonathan Clymer Photography
180-F Central Avenue
Englewood, NJ 07631
201-568-1760

Phil Degginger
Degginger Photography
9 Evans Farm Road
Morristown, NJ 07960
201-455-1733

Bruce Goldsmith
Bruce Goldsmith Photography
1 Clayton Court
Park Ridge, NJ 07656
201-391-4946

POCKET FOLDERS AND BINDERS

Mr. Jeff Becker
Clients First
90 Elm Street
Westfield, NJ 07090
908-232-1200

POWERPOINT PRESENTATIONS

Joyce Carmeli, Bonnie Blake,
  Mary Cicitta
Design On Disk
336 President Street
Saddle Brook, NJ 07663
973-253-2554

Prime Time Staffing
1250 East Ridgewood Avenue
Ridgewood, NJ 07450
201-612-0303

PREMIUMS AND INCENTIVES

Kimberly Lacey
Hanig & Company
1200 Business Center Drive, #400
Mount Prospect, IL 60056
847-699-9090

Nelson Marketing
210 Commerce Street
P.O. Box 320
Oshkosh, WI 54902-0320
800-982-9159

Perrygraf Slide Charts
19365 Business Center Drive
Northridge, CA 91324-3552
800-423-5329

Thomas M. Begg
Professional Concepts, Inc.
728 Lafayette Street
Paramus, NJ 07652
201-251-1822

PRINTING

Joe Pity
V&L Printing
Dumont, NJ 07628
201-384-9126

PROJECT AND TRAFFIC MANAGEMENT

Mr. Grant Faurot
92 Glendale Street
Nutley, NJ 07110
973-661-5074

PROJECT MANAGEMENT OUTSOURCING

Fern Dickey
Back Burner
9-16 Fourth Street
Fair Lawn, NJ 07410
201-797-9663

PROOFREADING

Debra Godfrey
Godfrey Editorial Services
3 Rush Court
Plainsboro, NJ 08536
609-936-0753
E-mail: dgodfrey@prodigy.net

Cynthia L. Shaw
3300 Neshaminy Blvd. #566
Bensalem, PA 19020
215-891-5165
E-mail: Cindy_lynne@msn.com

PUBLIC RELATIONS AGENCIES

Mr. Mark Bruce
GHB Marketing Communications
1177 High Ridge Road
Stamford, CT 06905
203-321-1242

Mr. Don Levin
Levin Public Relations
30 Glenn Street
White Plains, NY 10603
914-993-0900

George Whalen
G. J. Whalen & Company, Inc.
59 Lambert Road
New Rochelle, NY 10804-1009
914-576-6750

PUBLISHING ON DEMAND

James Bittker
ToExcel.com
37 Scarborough Park
Rochester, NY 14625
716-787-2092

RADIO COMMERCIALS

Chuck Hengel
Marketing Architects
14550 Excelsior Boulevard
Minneapolis, MN 55345
612-936-7500

RETAIL MARKETING

Neil Raphel
Raphel Marketing
12 South Virginia Avenue
Atlantic City, NJ 08401
609-348-6646

SELF-PROMOTION CONSULTANT

Ilise Benun
The Art of Self-Promotion
1012 Park Avenue Suite 6
Hoboken, NJ 07030
201-653-0783

SPEAKING COACHES AND CONSULTANTS

Somers White
4736 North 44th Street
Phoenix, AZ 85018
602-952-9292
Web site: www.somerswhite.com
E-mail: somerswhite@compuserv.com

STOCK ILLUSTRATIONS

Stock Illustration Source
16 West 18th Street
New York, NY 10011
212-691-6400
Web site: www.sisstock.com

TELEMARKETING

Grace Software Marketing
3091 Mayfield Road
Cleveland, OH 44118
216-321-2000

Frank Stetz
240 East 82 Street, 20th Floor
New York, NY 10028
212-439-1777

Mariann Weinstein
MAW Associates
115 North 10th Street
New Hyde Park, NY 11040
516-437-0529

TRADEMARK SEARCHES

American Trademark & Research
  Data
Web site: www.trademarkresearch.
  com

Thomson & Thomson
800-692-8833

TRANSLATIONS

Harvard Translations
137 Newbury Street
Boston, MA 02116
617-424-9291

TRAVEL SUPPLIES

Magellan's
110 West Sola Street
Santa Barbara, CA 93101-3007
800-962-4943

WEB PAGE DESIGN

Barry Fox
FoxTek
49 West Street
Northport, NY 11768
516-754-4304

Mr. Jason Petefish
Silver Star Productions
87 Aspen Ledges Road
Ridgefield, CT 06877
203-894-1849

Kent Martin
Network Creative
104 Mountain Avenue
Gilette, NJ 07930
908-903-9090

WORD AND DATA PROCESSING

Bob Bly
22 East Quackenbush Avenue,
3d Floor
Dumont, NJ 07628
201-385-1220
Fax: 201-385-1138
E-mail: rwbly@bly.com

PCM Data Processing
13-09 Berdan Avenue
Fair Lawn, NJ 07410
201-703-8860

Appendix F

Sample Documents

SAMPLE VIRUS PROTECTION POLICY

Explain to new and existing clients in a memo the steps you take to prevent the files you send them from being contaminated with viruses. Here is a sample antivirus protection policy.

To: All clients and potential clients

From: Bob Bly
        Center for Technical Communication
        22 East Quackenbush Avenue
        Dumont, NJ 07628
        201-385-1220

Re: Our antivirus policy
Last updated: 10-13-97
filename: VPOL

1. We make every effort to ensure that files sent to our clients via e-mail or disk are virus-free—but we *cannot* guarantee it.

2. We run McAfee 3.5 VirusScan, which is the most widely used antivirus program worldwide. It is used by 25 million people, 80 percent of the Fortune 1000, and 40,000 organizations.

3. According to McAfee, VirusScan technology has been shown in lab tests to detect virtually every virus. These include boot, file, multiparty, stealth, mutating, encrypted, and polymorphic viruses.

4. Since new viruses crop up all the time, we routinely upgrade our VirusScan program by downloading the latest versions from the McAfee BBS (bulletin board). We recommend that clients running VirusScan do likewise.

5. Even running the latest antivirus software cannot guarantee a virus-free file with absolute certainty, because of the new viruses being launched constantly. Clients should run the most recent version of whatever antivirus software they use.

6. If you open a file we sent you via e-mail and it contains a virus, that does *not* mean it had a virus when we sent it from our end: Files sent via the Internet can pick up files in transit.

7. The only 100 percent foolproof protection against receiving a virus is to request that documents be faxed instead of e-mailed. You can't pick up a virus from a hard copy.

8. If you have any problems with a virus in a file we send you, please notify us immediately: 201-385-1220. If you are having a virus problem in general, we can refer you to computer consultants who may be able to help.

Thanks,

Bob Bly

ONE-PAGE COURSE DESCRIPTION FOR AN IN-HOUSE CORPORATE TRAINING SEMINAR

Persuasive Presentations Skills for Technical Professionals

Making technical sales presentations is a difficult task. Often the audience is diverse, consisting of listeners at many different levels of technical competence and with different interests and objectives. Your challenge is to deliver the technical meat to the hardcore techies while giving less technical listeners the bottom-line information they need to make a decision in your favor. On top of that, many technical professionals are uncomfortable speaking before groups, making the task even tougher.

This seminar shows technical professionals how to make team and customer presentations that get their message across, build their credibility as an authority in the topic, and get the audience to trust them and want to do business with them. You'll discover how to make even the most seemingly boring subjects come alive for listeners by finding and focusing on the "kernel of interest" that connects their needs with the subject matter.

Contents

✔ Determining the exact topic of your talk.

✔ Researching your subject matter beyond your own knowledge.

✔ Organizing your material for maximum audience interest and appeal.

✔ How to grab and keep your audience's attention.

✔ How to determine—in advance—what the audience needs and wants to hear from you.

✔ Getting the audience to buy into your approach, technology, system, or solution.

✔ Creating, finding, and using visual aids that enhance rather than detract from your talk.

✔ What materials should you hand out—and when?

✔ Positioning the audience to take the next step.

✔ Answering questions—especially when you don't know the answer.

✔ Overcoming stage fright and gaining comfort and confidence when speaking to groups.

✔ Communicating one-on-one with your audience.

✔ Advanced tips to boost your presentation quality to the next level—quickly and easily.

Length of Program: One or Two Days.

The Center for Technical Communication (CTC), 22 East Quackenbush Avenue, Dumont, NJ 07628, phone 201-385-1220

SAMPLE CLIENT SATISFACTION SURVEY (POST-ASSIGNMENT)

To: Client
From: Bob Bly
Re: Performance evaluation
filename: Survey1

Dear Valued Client:

Would you please take a minute to complete and return this brief questionnaire to me? (Doing so is optional, of course.) It would help me serve you better—and ensure that you get the level of quality and service you want on every job. Thanks!

----

1. How would you rate the quality of the presentation I gave to your group?

   ❏ Excellent   ❏ Very good   ❏ Good   ❏ Fair   ❏ Poor

2. What overall rating would you give my services?

   ❏ Excellent   ❏ Very good   ❏ Good   ❏ Fair   ❏ Poor

3. How would you rate the value received compared with the fee you paid?

   ❏ Excellent   ❏ Very good   ❏ Good   ❏ Fair   ❏ Poor

4. What did you like best about my service?_____

5. What would you like to see improved? _____

Your name (optional) _____

Company_____

Please return this form to:

Bob Bly
22 East Quackenbush Avenue
Dumont, NJ 07628
Phone: 201-385-1220
Fax: 201-385-1138
E-mail: rwbly@aol.com

MEMO TO CLIENTS ADVISING THEM
THAT YOU ARE GOING ON VACATION

filename: VAC1

To: Clients and prospects
From: Carolyn Mazza, assistant to Bob Bly
Re: April schedule
Date: 3-20-00

Bob Bly will be traveling and out of the office April 21 to 25. He will be in touch with the office via voice mail. The office will be open during this period, and if you need anything, you can leave a voice mail for Bob at 201-385-1220, or call me directly at 201-703-8860. Let me know if you have any questions or need additional information.

SAMPLE LEAD GENERATING LETTER: IN-HOUSE CORPORATE TRAINING SEMINAR

Important News for Every Information Systems Professional Who Has Ever Felt Like Telling an End User, "Go to Hell"

Dear IS Manager:

It's ironic.

Today's users demand to be treated as *customers* of IS.

Yet many systems professionals don't have the customer service skills to make the relationship work.

Our training program, "Interpersonal Skills for IS Professionals," solves that problem by giving IS staff the skills they need to deal effectively with end users and top management in today's service-oriented corporate environment.

Presented jointly by The Center for Technical Communication and The Communication Workshop—two leaders in teaching "soft skills" to technical professionals—"Interpersonal Skills for IS Professionals" quickly brings your team to a new level in listening, negotiating, teamwork, customer service, and other vital skills for communicating complex systems ideas and technical processes to managers and end users.

Many leading companies—including IBM, AT&T, Symbol Technologies, Price Waterhouse, Cigna, American Airlines, Lever Brothers, Barnett Technologies, First Union, and Turner Broadcasting—count on us to help their technical professionals communicate more effectively and work more productively. You can, too.

For more information, including an outline of our "Interpersonal Skills for IS Professionals" program, just complete and mail the enclosed reply card. Or call 516-767-9590. You'll be glad you did.

Sincerely,

Gary Blake, Ph.D., Director

P.S. Reply now and we'll also send you a *free* copy of our new tip sheet, "The IS Professional's Guide to Improving Listening Skills." It will help everyone in your department gain a quicker, more accurate understanding of what users want, while helping to transform your customers from uninitiated end users into educated consumers who are easier and more reasonable to deal with.

(reply card)

YES, I'm interested in learning more about your on-site seminars in:

❏ "Interpersonal Skills for IS Professionals"
❏ "Technical Writing for Systems Professionals"

Name_____ Title _____

Company_____ Phone _____

Address _____

City _____ State _____ ZIP_____

❏ Call me now. Number of people requiring training:_____
❏ Call me in_____ (month/year)

For immediate information, call 516-767-9590
Or fax this card to 516-883-4006

SAMPLE LEAD-GENERATING LETTER: SELLING TRAINING SEMINAR TO A NICHE MARKET

Dear ≪Title≫ ≪LastName≫:

Your claims professionals are always on the firing line. They write important letters to the insured, attorneys, doctors, and other insurance companies. If those letters are ambiguous, vague, or disorganized or don't get to the point, your company could be in jeopardy. Customers may be lost . . . and so may court cases.

Last month, I ran four seminars in "Effective Business Writing for Claims Professionals" at Farm Bureau Insurance in Lansing, Michigan. According to Susan Earley, claims training analyst, "Because of our sessions with you . . . we are going to conduct a review of our form letters. Also, as our claims adjusters compose letters, their words will be friendlier and more clear to the person they're intended for—the reader!"

Couldn't your claims professionals benefit from writing better denial letters? Reservation-of-rights letters? Letters to insurance companies, doctors, and attorneys in which gaining specific information is vital?

I'm Gary Blake, and I'd like to help your claims professionals write better and faster. You may have seen my articles and ads in *Claims* magazine. Over the past 15 years, I've run writing seminars at more than 50 insurance companies, including Blue Cross/Blue Shield of Florida, Equitable, Maryland Casualty, and Liberty Mutual. By booking a one-day seminar, you'd be going a long way toward helping every claims adjuster, examiner, and representative in your department write better, be more productive, and keep more customers.

Sound interesting? If you'd like to learn more about how your department can benefit from this seminar, please call me at 516-767-9590, or return the enclosed caRoad

Sincerely,

Gary Blake, Director

This seminar is *completely customized* to claims professionals. Call me now and I'll send you my *free* "Eight Tips on Writing Better Claims Letters."

SAMPLE PRESS RELEASE

From: Bob Bly, 22 East Quackenbush Avenue, Dumont, NJ 07628
Contact: Bob Bly 201-385-1220

For immediate release

New Booklet Reveals 14 Proven Strategies for Keeping Businesses Booming in a Bust
Economy

New Milford, NJ—While some companies struggle to survive in a sluggish business environment, many do better than ever largely because they have mastered the proven but little-known strategies of "recession marketing."

That's the opinion of Bob Bly, an independent marketing consultant and author of the just-published booklet, "Recession Proof Business Strategies: 14 Winning Methods to Sell Any Product or Service in a Down Economy."

"Many business people fear a recession or soft economy, because when the economy is weak, their clients and customers cut back on spending," says Bly. "To survive in such a marketplace, you need to develop recession marketing strategies that help you retain your current accounts and keep those customers buying. You also need to master marketing techniques that will win you new clients or customers to replace any business you may have lost because of the increased competition that is typical of a recession."

Among the recession-fighting business strategies Bly outlines in his new booklet:

✔ *Reactivate dormant accounts.* An easy way to get more business is to simply call past clients or customers—people you served at one time but are not actively working for now—to remind them of your existence. According to Bly, a properly scripted telephone call to a list of past buyers will generate approximately one order for every 10 calls.

✔ *Quote reasonable, affordable fees and prices in competitive bid situations.* While you need not reduce your rates or prices, in competitive bid situations you will win by bidding toward the low end or middle of your price range rather than at the high end. Bly says that during a recession, your bids should be 15 to 20 percent lower than you would normally charge in a healthy economy.

✔ *Give your existing clients and customers a superior level of service.* In a recession, Bly advises businesses to do everything they can to hold on to their existing clients or customers, their "bread-and-butter" accounts. "The best way to hold on to your clients or customers is to please them," says Bly, "and the best way to please them is through better customer service. Now is an ideal time to provide that little bit of extra service or courtesy that can mean the difference between dazzling clients or customers and merely satisfying them."

✔ *Reactivate old leads.* Most businesses give up on sales leads too early, says Bly. He cites a study from Thomas Publishing which found that although 80 percent of sales to businesses are made on the fifth call, only one out of ten salespeople calls beyond three times. Concludes Bly: "You have probably not followed up on leads diligently enough, and the new business you need may already be right in your prospect files." He says repeated follow-up should convert 10 percent of prospects to buyers.

To receive a copy of Bly's booklet, "Recession Proof Business Strategies," send $8 ($7 plus $1 shipping and handling-to: Bob Bly, Dept. 109, 22 East Quackenbush Avenue, Dumont, NJ 07628. Cash, money orders, and checks (payable to "Bob Bly"-accepted. (Add $1 for Canadian orders.)

Bob Bly, an independent copywriter and consultant based in New Dumont, New Jersey, specializes in business-to-business, high-tech, and direct response marketing. He is the author of 18 books, including *How to Promote Your Own Business* (New American Library-and *The Copywriter's Handbook* (Henry Holt). A frequent speaker and seminar leader, Mr. Bly speaks nationwide on the topic of how to market successfully in a recession or soft economy.

Note: This press release generated 3,500 replies.

SAMPLE ARTICLE QUERY LETTER

You can promote yourself by publishing how-to and informational articles related to commercial writing in trade and business magazines read by your potential clients. To propose an article to an editor, use a query letter. The sample query below got me an assignment to write an article on letter-writing for *Amtrak Express* magazine—the magazine even paid me $400!

Mr. James A. Frank, Editor
Amtrak Express
34 East 51st Street
New York, NY 10022

Dear Mr. Frank:

    Is this letter a waste of paper?

    Yes—*if* it fails to get the desired result.

    In business, most letters and memos are written to generate a specific response: close a sale, set up a meeting, get a job interview, make a contact. Many of these letters fail to do their job.

    Part of the problem is that business executives and support staff don't know how to write persuasively. The solution is a formula first discovered by advertising copywriters—a formula called AIDA. AIDA stands for Attention, Interest, Desire, Action.

    First, the letter gets attention with a hard-hitting lead paragraph that goes straight to the point, or offers an element of intrigue.

    Then, the letter hooks the reader's interest. The hook is often a clear statement of the reader's problems, needs, concerns. If you are writing to a customer who received damaged goods, state the problem. And then promise a solution.

    Next, create desire. You are offering something—a service, a product, an agreement, a contract, a compromise, a consultation. Tell the reader the benefit he'll receive from your offering. Create a desire for your product.

    Finally, call for action. Ask for the order, the signature, the check, the assignment.

    I'd like to write a 1,500-word article on "How to Write Letters That Get Results." The piece will illustrate the AIDA formula with a variety of actual letters and memos from insurance companies, banks, manufacturers, and other organizations.

    This letter, too, was written to get a specific result—an article assignment from the editor of *Amtrak Express*.

    Did it succeed?

Regards,

Bob Bly

P.S. By way of introduction, I'm an advertising consultant and the author of five books including *Technical Writing: Structure, Standards, and Style* (McGraw-Hill).

SAMPLE PITCH LETTER TO
GET SPEAKING ENGAGEMENTS

Another excellent way to market yourself is by giving talks and speeches to groups of advertising and marketing professionals. Here's a model query letter you can use to generate such engagements:

Ms. Jane Smith
Program Director
Women in Engineering
Big City, USA

Dear Ms. Smith:

Did you know that, according to a recent survey in *Engineering Today*, the ability to write clearly and concisely can mean $100,000 extra in earnings over the lifetime of an engineer's career?

For this reason, I think your members might enjoy a presentation I have given to several business organizations around town, "Ten Ways to Improve Your Technical Writing."

As the director of Plain Language, Inc., a company that specializes in technical documentation, I have worked with hundreds of engineers to help them improve their writing. My presentation highlights the 10 most common writing mistakes engineers make, and gives strategies for self-improvement.

Does this sound like the type of presentation that might fit well into your winter program schedule? I'd be delighted to speak before your group. Please phone or write so we can set a date.

Regards,

Blake Garibaldi, Director
Plain Language, Inc.

LETTER TO ANSWER QUERIES
FROM NONPROSPECTS

As you spend time in this field, you will get inquiries from other speakers, wanna-be speakers, small businesses asking for free advice, and other nonprospects. I use this letter to respond to all these inquiries without having to make a phone call or write a personal letter.

I Really Hate Sending You This Letter, But . . .

Dear Colleague:

I like sending form letters even less than you like getting them. But sometimes it's necessary.

For example, I get enough calls and letters requiring a response that, if I were to personally answer them all, I'd have no time to get my work done. So rather than not answer at all, I've prepared this form response. Let's see if I can help you this way.

If you're like most of the people getting this letter, you're either of the following:

✔ A businessperson with questions about marketing and selling your products and services.

✔ A writer seeking help getting published or getting clients.

If this describes you, the information you need is available in one of three ways:

✔ *Publications.* Chances are the information you want is already in one of my books, reprints, or audiotapes. A publications catalog with order form is enclosed.

✔ *Quick phone chats.* I charge $250 an hour for my time. I'll gladly give you five minutes on the phone at no charge, but I can't set appointments for these chats. Call me at 201-385-1220, and if I'm there, we'll talk. If I'm not, leave a number where I can call you back collect.

✔ *Paid consultations.* If your problem requires more in-depth consultation, it's available on a limited basis for $250 an hour. However, I'm often booked to capacity, so my preference would be to have a quick no-charge chat or guide you to the appropriate book or report.

Thanks so much for writing. Let me know how else I can help you.

Sincerely,

Bob Bly

P.S. If there is any material enclosed with this letter in addition to my publications catalog, I sent it to you—at no cost—because I thought, based on your letter or call to me, that the information would be helpful to you. Enjoy!

SAMPLE PURCHASE ORDER

Excelsior Electronics, Inc.	Purchase Order	
1724 Industrial Avenue		
Voltage, Ohio 45333	Date:	
555-675-6657		
Issued to:	Authorized by:	
————————————	Ship via:	
————————————	Ship to attn.:	
————————————		
————————————		
Telephone Number:	by (date):	
Description	Price	
Purchase order number must appear on all invoices and correspondence. Please sign and return second and third copies.		
Signed:	Date:	

SAMPLE CONTRACT

Some consultants use simple contracts to confirm job assignments from clients. Here's one I have developed:

Contract for Consulting Services

From: Bob Bly   Phone: 201-385-1220
             22 East Quackenbush Avenue   Fax: 201-385-1138
             Dumont, NJ 07628

Date:

Client:

Job:

Fee:

Advance retainer required:

Balance due upon completion:

Notes:

Your signature below authorizes me to perform consulting services for the project described above, for the fee listed. Payment due net 30 days upon receipt of invoice.

Signed   _____

Title _____   Date _____

Please sign and return this form with your check for the amount listed under "Advance retainer required." This will give me the go-ahead I need to proceed with the assignment.

Note: If no retainer is required, you can save time by signing above and faxing the form back to me at 201-385-1138.

CONFIDENTIALITY AGREEMENT

Some clients may ask you to sign a confidentiality agreement saying you won't share the client's proprietary information with other people. If the client wants you to make such a promise but doesn't have their own confidentiality agreement, you can use a simple confidentiality memo as shown:

To: Sue Simon, ABC Systems
From: Bob Bly, phone 201-385-1220
Date: 12-11-96
Re: Nondisclosure agreement

1. "Confidential information" means any information given to me by ABC Systems.

2. I agree not to use, disseminate, or share any confidential information with my employees, vendors, clients, or anyone else.

3. I will use reasonable care to protect your confidential information, treating it as securely as if it were my own.

4. I won't publish, copy, or disclose any of your confidential information to any third party and will use my best efforts to prevent inadvertent disclosure of such information to any third party.

5. The copy I do for you shall be considered "work for hire." ABC Systems will own all rights to everything I produce for you, including the copyright. I will execute any additional documents needed to verify your ownership of these rights.

Sincerely,

Bob Bly

LETTER REQUESTING REFERRALS

One of the best sources of sales leads is referrals from existing clients. If your clients aren't giving you as many referrals as you want, here's a letter you can use to ask for more:

Ms. Joan Zipkin
Acme Retail Outlets
Anytown, USA

Dear Joan:

I'm glad you liked the seminar I recently gave to your fulfillment department. Like you, I'm always on the lookout for new business. So I have a favor to ask. Could you jot down, on the back of this letter, the names, addresses, and phone numbers of a few of your colleagues who might benefit from knowing more about my services?

(Naturally, I don't want anyone whose product line competes with your own.)

Then, just mail the letter back to me in the enclosed reply envelope.

I may want to mention your name when contacting these people. Let me know if there's any problem with that.

And thanks for the favor!

Regards,

Sam Tate

LETTER FOR SOLICITING TESTIMONIALS FROM CLIENTS

After completing a job successfully, you can use this letter to solicit a testimonial from the client. A sheet of paper filled with testimonials is a very powerful addition to a promotional package and convinces prospects you are good at what you do. I always send a self-addressed stamped envelope and two copies of the letter. This way the recipient doesn't have to make a copy of the letter or address and stamp his own envelope.

Mr. Andrew Specher, President
Hazardous Waste Management, Inc.
Anywhere, USA

Dear Andrew:

I have a favor to ask of you.

I'm in the process of putting together a list of testimonials—a collection of comments about my services from satisfied clients like yourself.

Would you take a few minutes to give me your opinion of my on-site training workshop? No need to dictate a letter, just jot your comments on the back of this letter, sign below, and return to me in the enclosed envelope. (The second copy is for your files.) I look forward to learning what you like about my service . . . but I also welcome any suggestions or criticisms, too.

Many thanks, Andrew.

Regards,

Bob Bly

You have my permission to quote from my comments, and use these quotations in ads, brochures, mail, and other promotions used to market your training services.

Signature_____   Date _____

LETTER FOR GETTING PERMISSION
TO USE EXISTING TESTIMONIAL

Some clients will send you letters of testimonial unsolicited. Before you use them in your promotions, get their permission in writing, using this form letter:

Mr. Mike Hernandez
Advertising Manager
Technilogic, Inc.
Anytown, USA

Dear Mike:

I never did get around to thanking you for your letter of 11/7/00 (copy attached). So . . . thanks!

I'd like to quote from this letter in the ads, brochures, direct mail packages, and other promotions I use to market my writing services—with your permission, of course. If this is okay with you, would you please sign the bottom of this letter and send it back to me in the enclosed envelope. (The second copy is for your files.)

Many thanks, Mike.

Regards,

Bob Bly

You have my permission to quote from the attached letter in ads, brochures, mail, and other promotions used to market your seminars and workshops.

Signature _____ Date _____

FOLLOW-UP FAX TO REACTIVATE INACTIVE CLIENT

From: Ilise Benun for Bob Bly
Phone: 201-385-1220

Dear

We try to practice what we preach and we know that it's good marketing practice to keep in touch with the clients we enjoy and want to work more closely with—clients like you.

Because we think there's a good fit between your needs and our skills, would you take a moment to tell us about your current or future training needs?

❑   We have an upcoming project. Give me a call.
❑   May have something within __next 6 months
    __6–12 months   __next year
❑   We're not using training services right now, but we'll keep you in our vendor file.
❑   No longer interested because   _____
    (Please give reason—thanks)

P.S. As a thank-you for responding, we'll send you a free copy of Bob's new book, *Quick Tips for Better Business-to-Business Marketing Communications*, recently published by the Business Marketing Association.

Fax back to: 201-385-1138
Or call: 201-385-1220

SAMPLE INVOICE

Here is a typical invoice to send a client upon completion of a job:

Invoice for Services Rendered

Date: July 15, 1999
From: David Willis
15 Sunnyville Drive
Anyplace, USA
123-555-1234
Social Security #XXX-XX-XXXX

To: XYZ Corporation
Anytown, USA
ATT: June Chapman, Advertising Manager

For: Half-day Personal Productivity Workshop 7/12/99

Reference: Purchase order #1745

Amount: $4,350

Training fee $4,000
Travel $350

Terms: net 30 days

Thank you.

SAMPLE COLLECTION LETTER SERIES

Letter #1

Dear Jim:

Just a reminder . . .

. . . that payment for the workshop I gave for you (see copy of invoice attached) is now past due.

Would you please send me a check today? A self-addressed stamped reply envelope is enclosed for your convenience.

Regards,

Bob Bly

Letter #2

Dear Jim:

I haven't gotten payment for this invoice yet. Did you receive my original bill and follow-up letter?

If there is any problem, please let me know. Otherwise, please send me a check for the amount due within the next few days.

Thanks,

Bob Bly

Letter #3

Dear Jim:

This is the third notice I've sent about the enclosed invoice, which is now many weeks past due.

Was there a problem with this class that I don't know about? When may I expect payment?

Sincerely,

Bob Bly

Letter #4

Dear Jim:

What do you think I should do?

Despite three previous notices about this invoice, it remains unpaid. I haven't heard from you, and you haven't responded to my letters.

Please remit payment within 10 days of receipt of this letter. I don't enjoy sending you these annoying notices, nor do I like turning accounts over to my attorney for collections. But you are leaving me little choice.

Sincerely,

Bob Bly

SAMPLE FACT SHEET: CONSULTING SERVICES

Bob Bly

Copywriter/Consultant/Seminar Leader

22 East Quackenbush Avenue, 3rd floor
Dumont, NJ 07628
Phone (201) 385-1220 • Fax (201) 385-1138

Marketing Communications Planning, Strategy, Consultation, and Copy

In today's economy, it pays to make every marketing communication count. But do yours?

From time to time, you've probably felt the need for help in planning, creating, and implementing effective direct mail, advertising, and public relations programs. For example, maybe you need advice and assistance in:

- Converting more leads to sales
- Generating more inquiries from print advertising
- Determining which vertical industries or narrow target markets to pursue
- Producing effective sales brochures, catalogs, case histories, and other marketing literature
- Writing and placing press releases, feature stories, and other publicity materials
- Creating response-getting direct mail offers, packages, and campaigns
- Designing, writing, and producing a company newsletter
- Or any of dozens of other marketing problems.

Maybe you've felt that the usual sources of assistance—freelancers, advertising agencies, and PR firms—were not focused on solving your particular problems, lacked the specific knowledge you require, didn't understand your product or service, charged unreasonable prices, or were not interested in your project because they wanted all your business.

Or maybe you just want some occasional guidance and assistance, and prefer to handle most of your marketing communications in-house.

> *Now there's a service designed especially to help you—*
> **Marketing Communications Planning, Strategy, and Consultation**
> *From Bob Bly—Copywriter/Consultant/Seminar Leader*

Here are some questions prospective clients typically ask me—and the answers:

What is the Marketing Communications Planning, Strategy, and Consultation Service? This is a service which assists small and medium-size firms in planning, creating, and implementing effective advertising, marketing, direct mail, publicity, and promotional programs. I act as your ongoing adviser, answering your questions, making recommendations, and providing whatever help you need to market and promote your product or service successfully.

How does it work? My service is flexible and available to you on whatever basis meets your needs. You can hire me by the project, by the day, by the hour, or on a flexible retainer basis. While I am happy to use our time in any way you like, I will always advise you on how I think you will get the best results for your money.

What is discussed between us? The topics range from the general to the specific. You can ask me basic information about direct mail or any other topic you want to know more about; or we can deal with the nuts-and-bolts specifics of any project you have in mind.

How is the service rendered? Most of my clients prefer to work by mail, phone, and fax. However, I am available to meet with you at your office or mine, and a number of my clients use a combination of face-to-face meetings and telephone conferences.

What aspects of marketing communications are you expert in? About 50 percent of my business is planning and writing direct mail campaigns. The rest involves planning and creating a wide assortment of marketing materials and programs including ads, brochures, feature articles, slide presentations, film and videotape scripts, press releases, newsletters, catalogs, case histories, annual reports, product guides, manuals, and speeches—in short, whatever you need to help you sell more of your products and services.

- over -

(Continued)

What industries do you specialize in? My specialties include business-to-business, industrial, high-tech, direct marketing, and financial services. Within these broad categories, I've worked with over a hundred clients in dozens of fields including computers, chemicals, pulp and paper, construction, electronics, engineering, industrial equipment, marine products, software, banking, health care, publishing, mail order, seminars, training, telecommunications, consulting, corporate, and many other areas. But that's just a sampling. If you want to know whether I have experience in your specific field, call me and I'll tell you.

What are some of the specific services you provide for clients? Clients have hired me to create marketing and advertising plans; review and discuss ongoing marketing activities; make recommendations on new ways to effectively market existing products and services; review and critique ads, mailings, and other marketing documents; plan and write direct mail campaigns; train in-house staff in copywriting and marketing; and simply be available to provide input, answer questions, or bounce around ideas.

What size companies do you work with? I work with small firms, medium-size companies, and divisions of large corporations. My service can be tailored to the complexity of your program and the size of your budget.

Do you actually implement recommendations? I am a copywriter and consultant, not an ad agency or design studio. I create marketing strategies and write copy, but I do not design, print, or produce the piece. If you need art or production services, I will refer you to qualified vendors in my network with whom you can work directly. This gives you greater control, faster delivery, and eliminates costly mark-ups on their services. I will be happy to review any work done for you by these or any other vendors you use (for example, many clients mail or fax rough layouts to me for comment before mechanicals are created).

Who will handle my account? All services are provided directly by Bob Bly. Mr. Bly is a well-known copywriter and consultant specializing in business-to-business and direct marketing. He has consulted with—and written copy for—more than 100 organizations including On-Line Software, Timeplex, Convergent Solutions, JMW Consultants, Associated Air Freight, Sony Corporation, Yourdon Inc., American Medical Collection Agency, Grumman, GE Solid State, and Philadelphia National Bank. He is the author of 20 books including *How to Promote Your Own Business* (New American Library), *Ads That Sell* (Asher Gallant), *The Copywriter's Handbook* (Henry Holt), *Create the Perfect Sales Piece* (John Wiley), *Direct Mail Profits* (Asher Gallant), and *Selling Your Services* (Henry Holt). A client list and publications catalog are available upon request.

What is the cost of Bob Bly's marketing consultation services? Clients can choose to be billed on an hourly, daily, retainer, or project basis. The base fee is $200 per hour.

What's the typical fee for new clients? I offer an introductory consultation for $900 which includes a review of your materials and questions, a 1-2 hour consultation (by phone, mail, or in-person), and a follow-up report outlining my recommendations. You get approximately 4 hours of consultation (a $1,000 value) for a package price of $600, so this is my best value.

Is all time billable? No. To see whether my service is right for you, I offer a free initial consultation by phone for 20 minutes. Thereafter, however, time is billable at $250 per hour.

Why would an organization choose Bob Bly's Marketing Communications Planning, Strategy, and Consultation Service over hiring a full-service agency? For at least three good reasons:

1) *Cost.* Most agencies won't help you unless they get your whole account and you spend at least $50,000 to $75,000 a year with them. I will help you solve your marketing problems within whatever budget constraints you set. Significant results can be achieved for as little as $900.

2) *Results.* Because my orientation is toward results, not aesthetics, many clients report an immediate increase in leads and sales after using my services. (Client testimonials available upon request.)

3) *Education.* As we work together, I teach you my techniques and strategies for boosting marketing communications effectiveness—so, over time, you learn to do more and more on your own.

What's the next step? Please call me at (201) 385-1220 and tell me how I can be of service. You may even want to schedule your free 20-minute telephone consultation to discuss how we can solve your most pressing marketing problems. Be sure to request your free Marketing Communications Audit, too.

Bob Bly • Copywriter/Consultant/Seminar Leader
22 East Quackenbush Avenue, 3rd floor • Dumont, NJ 07628
Phone (201) 385-1220 • Fax (201) 385-1138

SAMPLE PROMOTIONAL BROCHURE FOR AN INDEPENDENT CORPORATE TRAINER

THE CENTER FOR TECHNICAL COMMUNICATION

Technical and business writing seminars for corporations

In-house training programs

Public seminars

Conferences

Publications

The Technical Writing Hotline™

Fax Critique service

Train-the-trainer programs

Contract technical writing services

CTC Trainers Bureau

The Center for Technical Marketing

Everything you need to train your employees to write better and faster, boost productivity, and enhance the quality of your organization's written communications.

WHAT IS THE CENTER FOR TECHNICAL COMMUNICATION?

The Center for Technical Communication (CTC) is a company that specializes in improving the writing skills of corporate employees and the quality of written communications within your organization.

CTC's primary service is conducting in-house workshops in technical and business writing for corporate clients nationwide. Our on-site writing seminars give your employees the skills and confidence to write better, faster, and more productively.

CTC also offers public seminars, conferences, and publications covering all aspects of technical and business communication. Other services designed to improve the quality of communication in your organization include our telephone hotline, fax critique service, contract technical writing services, and more.

IN-HOUSE WRITING WORKSHOPS

CTC offers the following in-house training seminars for corporations and associations:

Effective Technical Writing

A 1 or 2-day workshop on how to write clear, correct, technically accurate reports, manuals, documentation, specs, proposals, papers, and other technical documents. This program is designed to improve the writing skills of engineers, scientists, systems analysts, technicians, technical writers, technical editors, and others whose writing deals with technical or semi-technical subject matter.

Effective Business Writing

A 1 or 2-day workshop on how to write clear, concise, persuasive letters, memos, reports, proposals, and other business documents. This program's focus is on improving the writing skills of executives, managers, professionals, and support staff.

Our instructors know technical writing because they are technicians and technical writers.

What sets CTC apart from other training firms is that our instructors are not only skilled and entertaining

trainers but are also *recognized authorities* in their fields. Our technical writing seminars, for example, are taught by instructors who hold technical degrees, have worked as full-time professional technical writers for large corporations, and have taught technical writing at the university level. In-depth experience and technical background not only improve the quality of instruction but also break down barriers between the instructor and the audience: Your technical trainees become more receptive when they realize the instructor is a "techie" like them.

PUBLIC SEMINARS AND CONFERENCES

Although CTC gives priority to meeting the in-house training needs of our corporate clients, we occasionally sponsor public seminars and conferences on technical and business writing. Companies with six or more people requiring training, however, will probably find an in-house program more cost-effective.

TRAIN-THE-TRAINER PROGRAM

Some companies do not have the budget to send as many of their employees as they'd like through our technical writing workshops. As a cost-effective alternative to on-site training, we offer a train-the-trainer program in which CTC licenses its course materials, including outlines and hand-outs, to you for use within your organization. We also coach your trainers in how to present our program effectively.

PUBLICATIONS

CTC offers books, special reports, monographs, and audio cassettes on a variety of topics including technical writing, marketing communications, and business communications.

THE TECHNICAL WRITING HOTLINE ™

This unique telephone hotline gives you instant access to technical writing experts who can provide immediate answers to questions concerning grammar, punctuation, spelling, usage, word choice, format, and style.

FAX CRITIQUE SERVICE

Clients can fax drafts to CTC for immediate review and editing. A qualified CTC technical editor reads the document, edits, provides further suggestions for improvement, and returns the original with corrections and comments to the client via fax.

CONTRACT TECHNICAL WRITING SERVICES

CTC maintains a large database of qualified technical writers with varied backgrounds and hourly rates. If your staff is overloaded and you need a technical writer, call CTC. We'll provide technical writers to work at your place or theirs on a project, hourly, or per diem basis. Should you wish to hire the writer full-time, CTC can arrange this through our Executive Search and Placement Division.

CTC TRAINERS BUREAU

In addition to staff instructors specializing in technical and business writing, CTC operates a trainers bureau providing trainers who fit your budget and can speak on such topics as:

- Business writing
- Technical writing
- Copywriting
- Persuasive writing for salespeople
- English as a second language
- Presentation skills
- Selling
- Direct mail/direct marketing
- Client service
- And many others.

THE CENTER FOR TECHNICAL MARKETING

The Center for Technical Marketing (CTM) is a division of CTC specializing in business-to-business, industrial, high-tech, and direct response marketing.

CTM creates award-winning, result-getting direct mail, packages, sales letters, brochures, ads, press releases, newsletters, data sheets, and other marketing documents for more than 100 clients nationwide.

CLIENTS (A PARTIAL LIST) *

Airco
Associated Distribution Logistics
Atech Software
Brooklyn Union Gas
Cambridge Scientific Abstracts
Chemical Bank
The Conference Board
Convergent Solutions
CoreStates Financial Corporation
Creative Group, Inc.
Crest Ultrasonics
Dow Chemical
Drake Beam Morin
EBI Medical Systems
Executive Enterprises
Fala Direct Marketing
Fielder's Choice
Grey Advertising
Howard Lanin Productions
IBM
IEEE
ITT
International Tile Exposition
The Institute of Management Accountants
JMW Consultants
J. Walter Thompson
Leviton Manufacturing
Metrum Instruments
Midlantic
M & T Chemicals
On-Line Software
Optical Data Corporation
Prentice Hall
PSE&G
Reed Travel Group
Sony
Siemens
Specialty Steel & Forge
Thompson Professional Publishing
Timeplex
Union Camp
Value Rent-a-Car
Wallace & Tiernan
Wolfram Research
And many, many others...

* The firms and associations listed have retained the seminar, training, writing or consulting services of CTC, Bob Bly, or The Center for Technical Marketing.

WHAT CLIENTS AND ATTENDEES SAY ABOUT CTC SEMINARS AND SERVICES...

" Thanks for the seminar. Besides clarifying technical points, you gave me insight into my position, and my abilities, as a writer. And observing you in action was excellent training. "

> — Mike Goldscheitter, technical writer
> *Loveland Controls*

" Thanks again for joining us in Atlantic City. I, and the entire group, found your thoughts insightful and right on target."

> — Edward H. Moore, editor
> *communication briefings*

" Your presentation for our seminar was sparkling, enthusiastic, and informative. The audience response was wonderful to see and hear. Our group benefited greatly and were quite vocal in their praise of you."

> — Wendy Ward, program chair
> *Women in Communications*

" The first issue of the spinal newsletter is enclosed. The sales force was very receptive to the newsletter and its contents. Thank you for helping us launch this important project. "

> — Mary Ellen Coleman, product manager
> *EBI Medical Systems*

" I just wanted to thank you personally for the energy and effort you put into your two days with us. We are now far better equipped to do direct mail for our clients and ourselves that will have a greater impact and get measurable results. "

> — Greta Bolger, account executive
> *Sefton Associates Inc.*

" I just finished reading the copy for our CERTIN-COAT system brochure and I was very happy with it. You did an excellent job of editing a large amount of information, much of it extraneous, into a strong, cohesive selling message."

> — Len Lavenda, advertising manager
> *M&T Chemicals Inc.*

" I found the seminar helpful and noticed a definite greater awareness of style afterwards. Your presentation was lively, and kept the participants' attention well into the afternoon and longer than I had expected beforehand."

> — J.E. Koschei, editorial director
> *Thompson Professional Publishing*

ABOUT CTC'S DIRECTOR

Bob Bly, director of the Center for Technical Communication, has been a technical writer and technical writing instructor full-time since 1979.

He taught technical writing at New York University and has presented training sessions to such groups as the American Chemical Society, the American Marketing Association, and the American Institute of Chemical Engineers.

Mr. Bly is the author of 25 books including *Technical Writing: Structure, Standards, and Style* (McGraw-Hill), *The Copywriter's Handbook* (Henry Holt), and *The Elements of Business Writing* (Macmillan).

Bob Bly has worked as a staff technical writer for the Westinghouse Electric Corporation and also as an independent technical writer handling projects for dozens of firms including Brooklyn Union Gas, Crest Ultrasonics, On-Line Software, and M&T Chemicals.

Mr. Bly holds a B.S. in engineering from the University of Rochester. He is a member of the Society for Technical Communication, American Institute of Chemical Engineers, and the American Society for Training and Development.

THE NEXT STEP

For more information on any of the services described in this brochure, or to discuss scheduling a technical writing or business writing seminar for your organization, call CTC at (201) 385-1220. Or write us today.

THE CENTER FOR TECHNICAL COMMUNICATION
22 E. Quackenbush Avenue
Dumont, NJ 07628
phone (201) 385-1220
fax (201) 385-1138

SAMPLE FOLDER COVER FOR
SPEAKER LITERATURE KIT

MAKE MORE
MONEY
(and spend less)
ON YOUR ...

Yellow-Pages Ad!

 Direct Mail!

Internet Advertising!

R I C H A R D
armstrong
Copywriter • Consultant • Speaker • Author

SAMPLE FOUR-PAGE SELF-MAILER
BROCHURE TO PROMOTE A PUBLIC SEMINAR

> "Learning how to write procedures and work instructions taught me about ISO 9000 and how powerful it really is."
> — Operations analyst

> "Handouts were specific examples of what to do and what not to do. The exercises made understanding the material easy and comfortable. Excellent."
> — QA Engineer

> "The specifics were great. The most frustrating part of ISO documentation is vagueness. Also, where does a company begin? You covered this very well."
> Technical Writer

A comprehensive 2-day seminar
WRITING FOR ISO 9000

How to write quality manuals, procedures, work instructions, and other documentation required for ISO 9000 certification

Led by Gary Blake and Robert W. Bly, co-authors of the best-selling writing books, *The Elements of Technical Writing* and *The Elements of Business Writing*.

Getting ISO certified can produce dramatic improvements in quality while giving your company a competitive edge in today's global marketplace. But getting ISO certified isn't easy.

When it comes to the quality, clarity, and context of your writing, ISO 9000 auditors hold your company to a strict standard.

Since 1982, Blake and Bly have helped more than 45,000 managers, engineers, and professionals nationwide improve their writing. Now your team members can learn how to write clear, concise, accurate documentation to ensure that your company gets ISO certified.

Program includes:

- The 4 key ingredients of successful ISO documentation

- How to organize and prepare ISO quality manuals

- Making your ISO 9000 documents "auditor friendly"

- The worst mistake you can make in writing quality documents

- Real-life examples of quality manuals, procedures, and work instructions

- How to edit and improve your company's documentation

Locations and dates:

- Fort Lee, NJ   *Days Inn*   October 26 - 27, 1994
- Chicago, IL   *The Palmer House*   November 15 - 16, 1994
- San Jose, CA   *Le Baron*   January 25 - 26, 1995

"Writing for ISO 9000" is jointly sponsored by: THE CENTER FOR TECHNICAL COMMUNICATION

THE
COMMUNICATION WORKSHOP

Conforming to ISO 9000 quality standards requires quality writing. But do your team members write as well as they can?

At last! A writing seminar specifically designed for companies seeking ISO 9000 accreditation...

"Writing For ISO 9000"
How to write quality manuals, procedures, work instructions, and other documentation required for ISO 9000 certification

A comprehensive 2-day seminar

Benefits of taking the "Writing for ISO 9000" program

You and your team members will:

- Walk away with an armload of sample quality manuals, procedures, and work instructions written by other companies seeking ISO accreditation

- Understand what ISO 9000 is, how it works, and what auditors really look for when reviewing quality documentation

- Pinpoint flaws in current documentation and make major improvements that dramatically increase your chances of passing your ISO audit

- Gain an understanding of how other organizations create, edit, review, present, and manage their ISO documentation

- Prevent wordy, vague, ambiguous, and poorly written documentation from becoming a barrier to achieving ISO certification

- Create clear, concise, easy-to-understand quality documentation that meets with auditor approval and reduces the cost of certification

- Have your employees write better, faster, and with greater confidence and enjoyment

"Writing for ISO 9000"—Course Contents

Module I: ISO 9000 overview
* What are the ISO 9000 standards and where can you obtain them?
* 14 benefits of pursuing ISO 9000 accreditation
* Plain-English explanations of the various ISO 9000 standards
* 10 steps to ISO certification

Module II: Principles of writing clear, concise ISO documentation
* 10 key principles of writing for ISO 9000
* 4 things ISO registrars look for when reviewing documentation
* How to write numbers, units, equations, and symbols
* Why wordiness costs you money — and how to be more concise
* Techniques for editing and improving existing documentation
* The 4 basic types of documentation required for ISO 9000 — and how to distinguish between them

Module III: Writing quality manuals
* What is a "quality manual"?
* How to organize and outline your quality manual
* How to make your quality manual "auditor friendly"
* Referencing other documentation in your quality manual
* How specific and detailed should the quality manual be?
* Ideal page length and format for quality manuals
* Developing an action plan for getting your manual written
* Model outlines for ISO quality manuals
* Creating effective numbering blocks and headers for quality manuals
* Review and critique of sample quality manuals

Module IV: Writing procedures
* What is a procedure?
* Principles of procedure writing

* Headings that every procedure should contain
* Who should be the author of a procedure?
* How to get plant personnel to cooperate in the writing process
* Maximum number of steps that should be in a procedure
* Must your procedures include flow charts or other visuals?
* Proper format — spacing, title block, approvals, numbering, revisions
* Review, critique, and editing of sample procedures

Module V: Work instructions
* What is a work instruction?
* What are the differences between a work instruction and a procedure?
* The 7 key sections of a work instruction
* Review, critique, and editing of sample work instructions
* How to create effective records and forms

Module VI: Making your ISO 9000 documentation perfect
* Principles of effective technical composition
* Correct usage of grammar and punctuation
* Tips on proper capitalization and spelling
* A glossary of commonly used ISO terms
* Bibliography of books, articles, and publications dealing with ISO 9000
* Listing of U.S. ISO 9000 registrars

FACT: Almost 70 percent of manufacturers fail their initial ISO audit. Learn how to improve your documentation — and help your company gain ISO 9000 certification sooner and at less cost.

FACT: According to an article in the *Record*, 80 percent of all businesses want their key vendors to be ISO 9000 certified. And that number is increasing weekly.

What attendees are saying about "Writing for ISO 9000"...

"I liked everything, especially the detail on procedures and work instructions and helpful guidelines on writing skills."
—Quality assurance coordinator

"I liked the specific examples from the world of industry about ISO registration activities. Fast-paced — didn't get boring."
—Quality assistant

"Helped me learn how to write procedures and policy manuals that conform to ISO 9000."
—QA specialist

"Excellent interaction with attendees. You guys fielded all questions like pros."
—QA manager

"Reviewing and editing different documents was most effective."
—Metallurgical engineer

"I liked reviewing forms for corrections to make me more aware. The interaction with others was also very good."
—Plant manager

"Interaction with the instructors and other participants was quite helpful. The overview presented was both positive and informative. The use of multimedia helped keep attention."
—Plating manager

"Specific examples were given. The information can be used to help me write my documentation."
—Director of quality assurance

"The use of examples and critiquing these examples was very helpful."
—Quality systems engineer

About your seminar leaders...

Dr. Gary Blake is the director of The Communication Workshop, a Port Washington, NY firm that teaches technical and business writing. His latest book, *Quick Tips for Better Business Writing*, will be published next year by McGraw-Hill.

Bob Bly is the director of The Center for Technical Communication, a Dumont, NJ firm that teaches technical writing and writes technical documents for clients nationwide. Mr. Bly holds a B.S. in engineering and was a technical writer for Westinghouse.

Course materials

Each workshop participant will receive at no extra cost:

* A copy of Blake and Bly's best-selling book, *The Elements of Technical Writing*
* One year's free use of the Technical Writing Hotline
* One month's free use of our "Editing by Fax" editorial service
* Definitions of ISO 9000 standards
* Numerous samples of quality manuals, procedures, and work instructions from companies that have obtained or are in the process of seeking ISO accreditation

Here are just some of the organizations that have sent their employees to attend "Writing for ISO 9000"

AluChem Inc.
Bartech Inc.
Bostek, Inc.
Cabot Medical
Cardone Industries
CitiSteel USA
Clark Filter
Coca-Cola Foods
Dana Corp.
Dynepco, Inc.
Hil-Rom Co.
Johnston Corporation
Lau Corp.

Louis Dreyfus District Center
Mound Applied Technologies
Peerless Tube Co.
PMI Food Equipment
Powell Electronics
Purepack Pharmaceuticals
Roy F. Weston Co.
Sealtron
Technitrol
The Trane Company
U.S. Mint
U.S. Navy

About the seminar sites

* **Fort Lee, NJ.** Days Inn. Only 5 minutes from New York City.

* **Chicago, IL.** Palmer House. Right in the heart of downtown Chicago.

* **San Jose, CA.** Le Baron Hotel. Only 1/2 mile from the airport

All hotels have swimming pools, and most are equipped with exercise rooms. All are conveniently located, allowing you to enjoy the night life and sights of the city.

A comprehensive 2-day seminar

WRITING FOR ISO 9000

How to write quality manuals, procedures, work instructions,
and other documentation required for ISO 9000 certification

Registration Information

Fees: $595 per person. The fee includes professional
instruction, all course materials, and refreshments.
Food and lodging are not included.

Class size: The course is limited to 25 participants.

Payment: Payment is due prior to the workshop date.
Registration permitted the day of the seminar on a space-
available basis only.

Cancellation: If cancellation is made at least 10 days
prior to the workshop, your money will be refunded in
full. Otherwise, the entire fee will be applied to a future
program of your choice. You may send another participant in your place, if you wish.

Lodging: For room reservations, call the hotel directly.
NJ: Days Inn (201) 944-5000. *IL:* Palmer House Hilton
(312) 726-7500. *CA:* LeBaron (408) 453-6200.

In-House Training Programs

If you have 8 or more people to train, an in-house training seminar in "Writing for ISO 9000" might be a better choice for
you. You'll save money, have the course totally customized to your ISO certification efforts at no extra cost, and can critique
ISO documentation in the comfort and privacy of your own offices. For more information on in-house programs, call The
Communication Workshop at (516) 767-9590.

How to Register

By phone: Call (516) 767-9590 to
reserve space.
Charge it to your American Express
card, if you wish.

By mail: Complete and return the
registration form below.

By fax: Complete the registration
form and fax to (516) 883-4006

- -

Yes! **Please register me and the following participants for "Writing for ISO 9000"**

❑ Confirms telephone registration already made

I will attend in this city:

❑ Fort Lee, NJ *Days Inn* October 26-27, 1994

❑ San Jose, CA *Le Baron* January 25-26, 1995

❑ Chicago, IL *The Palmer House* November 15-16, 1994

Name_____ Title_____

Name_____ Title_____

Name_____ Title_____

Name_____ Title_____

Company_____ Phone_____

Address_____ Mail Code_____

City_____ State_____ Zip_____

The cost is $595 per person.

Method of payment.

❑ Check payable to "The Communication Workshop" enclosed

❑ Please charge my American Express.

     Card No._____

     Sig._____ Exp. date_____

❑ Please bill me. Our PO number is:_____

Bulk Rate
U.S. Postage
PAID
Permit No. 70
Westwood, NJ

Send this form and payment to:
The Communication Workshop
130 Shore Road
Port Washington, NY 11050
Phone (516) 767-9590 / Fax (516) 883-4006

SAMPLE MINICATALOG OF INFORMATION PRODUCTS (RELATED TO CONSULTING SPECIALTY)

Bob Bly's
Sales and Marketing Resource Guide™

Books, special reports, audio tapes, and other resources to help you communicate more effectively, improve marketing results, and sell more of your products and services.

Cassette programs (800-Series)

803　How to Boost Your Direct Mail Response Rates
Proven techniques for dramatically increasing your direct mail response rates. Includes rules for testing, target marketing strategies, offers, list selection, design, copy, mistakes to avoid...and much, much more.
Single cassette $12

804　Sixteen Secrets of Successful Small Business Promotion
How to use low-cost/no-cost advertising, marketing, sales promotion, and public relations techniques to build your business. Learn how to: Gain credibility through public speaking. Generate thousands of leads using simple press releases. The "Busy Doctor" Success Strategy. Resource boxes. Big results from tiny ads. Telephone hotlines. Client newsletters. And more.
Single cassette $12

805　Selling Your Services in a Soft Economy
How to successfully sell and market your service or product in a recession or soft economy.
Single cassette $12

806　How to Write Copy That Sells
Tips on writing result-getting copy for ads, direct mail, and other marketing communications.
Single cassette $12

807　The 7 Fundamental Shifts in Your Customer's Buying Habits in the 1990's
Corporate and consumer customers buy differently today than when the economy was stronger. You need to adjust your marketing and selling to meet the buyer's new shopping habits. This tape shows how.
Single cassette $12

808　Twelve Things You Can Do to Sell More of Your Products and Services—NOW!
Tips on prospecting, qualifying, closing, and improving overall sales results.
Single cassette $12

809　How to Become a Published Author
Why writing a book can enhance your career—and how to get your book published. Covers literary agents, advances, royalties, book contracts, and more.
Single cassette $12

810　How to Create Effective Seminar Brochures
Guidelines for writing and designing brochures to sell public and in-house seminars.
Single cassette $12

812　The Motivating Sequence
A proven, easy-to-follow 5-step formula for writing more persuasive sales letters, billing series, ads, mailers, and more.
Single cassette $12

813　Secrets of Successful Lead Generation
How to make your ads, sales letters, and mailers generate more leads.
Single cassette $12

814　Conversations on Getting and Keeping Customers
Two in-depth radio interviews with Bob Bly on the topics of selling and customer service.
Single cassette $12

815　How to Create Great Promotional Literature
12 tips on how you can create and use sales literature and other promotional materials more effectively.
Single cassette $12

Full-length books (300-Series)

300　Get Paid to Write Your Book
The definitive work on how to write a nonfiction book and sell it—for a nice advance—to a major New York publishing company. Topics include: coming up with book ideas, evaluating the market potential of your book, how to write a successful book proposal, how to get a literary agent to represent you, selling your book to publishers, and negotiating your advance and royalties.
Oversize paperback, 100 pages $22

301　The Copywriter's Handbook
The Copywriter's Handbook tells you how to write, commission, review, edit, and approve effective copy for ads, brochures, catalogs, direct mail, press releases, TV and radio commercials, newsletters, speeches, and other projects—with the emphasis clearly on business-to-business, industrial, hi-tech, and direct response. "I don't know a single copywriter whose work would not be improved by reading this book," says David Ogilvy, founder of Ogilvy & Mather. "And that includes me." Also recommended by The Los Angeles Times and Ad Day.
Updated trade paperback edition, 353 pages $15

305　The Elements of Technical Writing
A fully revised, completely updated edition of our 1982 bestseller, *Technical Writing: Structure, Standards, and Style*. Presents the guidelines and rules of technical writing in a concise, clear, easy-to-follow handbook, organized for quick and easy reference.
Hardcover, 144 pages $21

306　Creative Careers: Real Jobs in Glamour Fields
A job-hunter's guide to ten of today's most exciting industries including advertising, television, gourmet foods, finance, music, publishing, film, photography, theater, and travel.
Trade paperback, 334 pages $12

307　Create the Perfect Sales Piece: A Do-It-Yourself Guide to Producing Brochures, Catalogs, Fliers, and Pamphlets
Provides step-by-step instructions on how to successfully outline, plan, write, design, and produce sales brochures, booklets, fliers, pamphlets, annual reports, catalogs, and other collateral materials. Also contains model outlines for product, service, and corporate capabilities brochures.
Trade paperback, 242 pages $20

313　How To Promote Your Own Business
A practical, do-it-yourself guide to advertising, publicity, and promotion for the small-business manager or owner. Written especially for the small and medium-size firm (or division of a larger company) with a limited budget for advertising and marketing.
Trade paperback, 241 pages $13

315　Selling Your Services: Proven Strategies for Getting Clients to Hire You (or Your Firm)
If you sell professional, personal, consulting, trade, technical, support, or any other kind of service, this book will give you the information you need to get large numbers of prospects to call you, convince those prospects to hire you at the fees you want, and dramatically increase the sales of your services.
Hardcover, 349 pages $27

Full-length books (300-Series), cont'd

316 The Elements of Business Writing
The Elements of Business Writing presents the basic rules of business writing in a concise, easy-to-use handbook organized along the lines of Strunk and White's classic book, *The Elements of Style.*
Hardcover, 140 pages $20

317 Business-to-Business Direct Marketing
This book is for business-to-business marketers who want to improve results from all their marketing communications including ads, direct mail, PR, brochures, catalogs, postcard decks, and more. Also identifies and explains the 7 key differences between b-to-b and consumer marketing.
Hardcover, 267 pages $42

318 Targeted Public Relations
A no-nonsense guide to achieving maximum visibility, press coverage, leads, and sales from public relations done on a limited budget.
Hardcover, 330 pages $25

319 Keeping Clients Satisfied
In today's economy, clients and customers are more demanding than ever: They want it better, they want it cheaper, and they want it *yesterday!* This book shows you the customer service techniques necessary to satisfying and retaining clients in this new competitive mar etplace where the client reigns supreme.
Hardcover, 275 page $27

323 The Advertising Manager's Handbook
A comprehensive instruction manual on how to plan, implement, and manage an advertising and marketing communications program. Written from the advertising manager's point of view, the *Handbook* is recommended for *anyone* involved in producing, managing or evaluating marketing communication.
Hardcover, 800 pages $80

324 How to Sell Your House, Co-op, or Condo
Selling your house or apartment? Want to get it sold quickly at a good price? This book tells how.
Trade paperback, 242 pages $17

325 The Ultimate Unauthorized Star Trek Quiz Book
More than 750 trivia questions to test your "Trekpertise." covers the Star Trek movies, TV shows, and novels.
Trade paperback, 162 pages $11

326 Power-Packed Direct Mail
Complete, easy-to-follow instructions on how to increase direct mail response rates. Covers planning, offers, mailing lists, testing, copy, design, formats, personalizations, and more.
Hardcover, 349 pages $27

Reprints, monographs, booklets, and special reports (100-Series)

101 Thirty-One Ways to Get More Inquiries From Your Ads
Proven, easy, inexpensive strategies for increasing your ad's pulling power and getting more leads from each insertion.
1-page reprint $1

102 Using Testimonials To Improve Your Marketing Communications
Using testimonials is one of the easiest and most effective ways to add interest and credibility to marketing documents and make them more persuasive. This reprint tells how to get testimonials, how to use them, and provides model letters for soliciting testimonials and getting approval for publication.
2-page reprint $2

103 How To Prepare For a Copywriting Assignment
A four-step procedure for gathering the information you or your agency will need to write persuasive, meaningful copy. Includes

a checklist of 20 questions to ask before you write your ad or brochure.
1-page reprint $1

104 Marketing To Engineers
What works in advertising aimed at engineers—and what doesn't—is concisely spelled out in this report. Should industrial advertising mimic consumer advertising—or should it be more technical? Send for this tip sheet and find out....
1-page reprint $1

105 How To Sell Software By Mail
How to sell software using direct response space ads, direct mail packages, and sales brochures. Tells: How to select your offer based on the list price of the software. Proper use of demo diskettes. One-step vs. two-step promotions. And more.
2-page reprint $2

106 Creating Effective Sales Brochures For Technical Products
Five industry experts—including Terry Smith of Westinghouse and Dick Hill of Alexander Marketing—reveal their secrets for creating effective technical sales literature.
6-page reprint $4

107 In Search of Ink: How To Write a Feature Article or Case History and Get It Published
A step-by-step, proven procedure for writing business and technical articles and getting them published in trade journals. Includes interviews with top trade journal editors who tell what they like (and don't like) about PR agencies, PR managers, outlines, query letters, sloppy manuscripts, authors, and more.
4-page reprint $3

108 The Twelve Most Common Direct Mail Mistakes—and How To Avoid Them
How many of the 12 most common direct mail mistakes are you making right now? Even one could kill the response to your next mailing. Learn how to avoid these costly mistakes and create effective direct mail that generates lots of leads and orders!
4-page reprint $3

109 Recession-Fighting Business Strategies That Work
14 proven techniques for successfully selling and marketing your product or service in a recession, soft economy, or when business is slow.
16-page booklet $7

110 Twenty-Five Japanese Business Secrets
Most of what you need to know about doing business with the Japanese is covered in this insightful insider's briefing by Milt Pierce.
8-page report $6

111 Ten Ways to Improve Your Technical Writing
Ten tips for more effective technical communication. How to overcome Writer's Block. Nine ways to organize your writing. And more.
4-page reprint $3

112 Tips for Marketing High-Tech Products
Eight useful ideas for getting more response from marketing communications designed to promote high-tech products and services.
2-page reprint $2

113 The Key to Great Inquiry Fulfillment
How to put together a winning inquiry fulfillment package that gives the prospects the information they need and convinces them to take the next step in the buying process.
4-page reprint $3

114 Adventures in the Seminar Trade
How to make money in the public seminar business. How to promote your product or service using free seminars.
2-page reprint $2

BBL-520.11

115   How to Write and Sell Your Nonfiction Book
How to write and organize your book...write a winning book proposal...get a literary agent...sell your book to a publisher...book contracts...royalties and advances...and more.
2-page reprint $2

116   How to Set (and Get) Your Fees
Presents a simple formula for setting your fees. Helps you avoid charging too little (which can hurt your image and limit income) or too much (which can blow potential clients away and cost you sales).
2-page reprint $1

117   Writing Catalog Copy That Sells
Proven techniques for organizing and writing catalog copy that sells. A collection of my best columns from the Sroge newsletter on catalog marketing.
10-page report $6

118   Fifty Lead-Generating Tips
50 proven techniques for increasing response to lead-generating direct mail.
1-page reprint $1

119   Twenty-two Rules for Successful Self-Promotion
22 marketing tips for freelancers, consultants, and other self-employed professionals who market their services, plus 5 techniques for generating new business leads using direct mail.
2-page reprint $2

120   How to Give a Successful Speech or Presentation
More than 40 sensible suggestions on how to organize, write, and deliver an effective, memorable lecture, talk, speech, or presentation.
3-page reprint $2

121   The 29 Types of Article You Can Include in Your Company Newsletter
Wondering what to put in a company newsletter? Here are 29 types of stories you can use.
1-page reprint $1

122   How to Write a Good Advertisement
The 8 characteristics of a successful print ad. Plus: 7 ways to create business publication ads that get results.
2-page reprint $1

123   How to Sell "Information Products" By Mail
Tips on how to sell books, newsletters, special reports, audio cassettes, videos, monographs, and other "information products" successfully by mail.
1-page reprint $1

124   Videos and Audio Cassettes as a Marketing Tool
How to use audio cassettes and videotapes as a marketing tool to increase response to direct mail, ads, inquiry fulfillment, etc.
2-page reprint $2

125   How to Hire a Freelance Copywriter
7 key questions to ask before you hire a freelance copywriter.
1-page reprint $1

126   How to Present Your Product's or Service's Features and Benefits
Should you stress features? benefits? both? how? This reprint shows how to achieve the right balance when describing features and their benefits in your copy.
2-page reprint $2

127   Designing an Effective Outer Envelope
Answers "Should I use a teaser?", "First-class or third-class?", "Stamp, meter, or indicia?", "Label, window, or inkjet?" and other commonly asked questions about designing outer envelopes so that the direct mail package will be opened instead of thrown away.
1-page reprint $1

128   Creating a Successful Corporate Capabilities Brochure
4 main functions of corporate literature. 4 questions to ask before you create your company brochure. 10 tips for creating more effective capabilities brochures.
4-page reprint $3

129   Ten Ways to _Stretch_ Your Advertising Budget
Proven money-saving techniques from a master miser for stretching your marketing communications budget in today's economy.
2-page reprint $2

130   Taking the Mystery Out of High-Tech Direct Mail
How to increase response rates to direct mail packages designed to sell software, computers, and other high-tech products and services.
4-page reprint $3

131   Ten Ways to Improve Your Trade Show Direct Mail
How to create mailings that get more qualified prospects to visit your booth
3-page reprint $2

132   Twenty-Three Tips for Improving Your Business-to-Business Direct Mail
The title says is all. First published in Who's Mailing What.
4-page reprint $2

133   Premiums for Subscription Promotions
Five experienced circulation directors discuss how to select and test premiums for subscription promotion.
7-page reprint $3

134   Using Direct Mail to Promote Consulting and Professional Services
5 tips on generating leads for consulting and professional services using direct mail.
1-page reprint $1

135   The Seven Key Differences Between Business-to-Business and Consumer Marketing
At last, an authoritative answer to the long-standing debate, "Are business-to-business and consumer marketing the same, or different?"
3-page reprint $2

136   How to Write Business Letters that Get Results
Tips for writing more effective letters and memos.
4-page reprint $2

137   Ten Direct Mail Copywriting Tips
How to write potent copy that generates more leads and sales by mail.
4-page reprint $2

138   Ten Ways to Improve Your Copywriting
10 controversial suggestions on how to improve your copy by breaking the conventions.
3-page reprint $2

139   How to Review, Approve, and Critique Copy from Your Freelancer or Agency
Outlines the proper way to review, approve, and make changes to copy written by others.
2-page reprint $1

140   Ten Tips for Writing Better User Manuals
Ideas for creating software documentation that's easy to use.
2-page reprint $2

141   Practical Techniques for Producing Profitable Ideas
9 steps toward enhancing your creative thinking and coming up with better ideas.
2-page reprint $2

142   Eight Ways to Improve Your Managerial Skills
Tips for becoming a more effective manager.
2-page reprint $1

Reprints, monographs, booklets, and special reports (100-Series), cont'd

143 Improving Your Listening Skills
Tells how to become a better listener.
2-page reprint $1

144 Improving Your Time Management Skills
Common-sense (but often ignored) ways to gain control of your schedule and make more productive use of your time.
1-page reprint $1

145 Improving Your Telephone Skills
Guidelines on telephone etiquette to help you make the right impression with customers, prospects, colleagues, and other callers.
2-page reprint $1

146 Improving Your Technical Writing Skills
How to overcome anxiety and write more effectively using the TAP and SPP formulas.
2-page reprint $1

147 Improving Your "People Skills"
Tips on getting along with others and coping with difficult people.
2-page reprint $1

148 Improving Your Negotiating Skills
How to be less afraid, more assertive, ask for what you want, and get it a lot of the time.
2-page reprint $1

149 Ten Ways to Reduce Stress
Ten proven techniques for coping with work-related pressure.
1-page reprint $1

150 Twelve Ways to Improve Your Reading Efficiency
Strategies for reading faster while increasing comprehension and retaining more of what you've read.
1-page reprint $1

151 Negotiate Your Way to a Better Salary
9 strategies to help you ask for and get a raise.
1-page reprint $1

152 Job Burnout
The causes and cures. How to enjoy work again.
3-page reprint $2

153 On-Target Advertising
10 steps to creating ads that work.
5-page reprint $1

154 Out On Your Own: From Corporate to Self-Employment
What to do if you want to quit your job (or are fired) and start your own business.
2-page reprint $1

155 Ten Tips for Writing More Effective Industrial Copy
Copywriting tips for industrial trade ads, brochures, data sheets, and catalogs.
2-page reprint $2

156 Marketing Chemicals and Chemical Equipment
How to use advertising and publicity to market chemicals and process equipment. Contains sample press releases, sales letters, and a list of chemical publications.
30-page reprint $12

Dear Business Professional:

If you want affordable solutions to your sales and marketing problems, here's a valuable resource for you.

The **Sales and Marketing Resource Guide** gives you access to virtually everything I've written on sales, marketing, management, and business communication, including all of my books and articles, plus tapes of my seminars and speeches. Specific, relevant, practical information on key issues of interest to you is available in a variety of formats, for as little as $1. That's a bargain you can't beat anywhere.

Have a question? Call me at (201) 385-1220. As always, there's no charge for me to answer brief questions about something you've read in my books or articles. If your need is more complex and requires more extensive attention, I'll tell you what's involved and what it would cost for me to work with you. No obligation, of course.

—Bob Bly

Clip this coupon and mail it with your payment. (You may photocopy it, if you wish.)

Items you wish to order (indicate item #'s): _____ _____

_____ _____ _____ _____

_____ _____ _____ _____

_____ _____ _____ _____

Name _____ Title _____

Company _____ Phone _____

Address _____

City _____ State _____ Zip _____

❑ Check here if you would like to receive free, no-obligation information on my copywriting and consulting services. (If you have an immediate need, call Bob Bly at 201-385-1220.)

Enclose money order, cash, or check (payable to "Bob Bly") for appropriate amount. NJ residents add 6% sales tax. Canadian residents add $2 (U.S. dollars) per order. 30-day money-back guarantee on all books and cassettes. All items guaranteed to please. We require payment with order and do not accept purchase orders.

Mail to: **Bob Bly, 22 East Quackenbush Avenue, 3rd floor, Dumont, NJ 07628**   BBL-520.11

SAMPLE NEEDS ASSESSMENT FORM

Bob Bly's
Business-to-Business
Marketing Communications Audit

In today's economy, it pays to make every marketing communication count.

This simple audit is designed to help you identify your most pressing marketing communications challenges—and to find ways to solve problems, communicate with your target markets more effectively, and get better results from every dollar spent on advertising and promotion.

Step One: Identify Your Areas of Need

Check all items that are of concern to you right now:

❑ Creating a marketing or advertising plan

❑ Generating more inquiries from my print advertising

❑ Improving overall effectiveness and persuasiveness of print ads

❑ Determining which vertical industries or narrow target markets to pursue

❑ How to effectively market and promote our product or service on a limited advertising budget to these target audiences

❑ Producing effective sales brochures, catalogs, and other marketing literature

❑ How to get good case histories and user stories written and published

❑ Getting articles by company personnel written and published in industry trade journals

❑ Getting editors to write about our company, product, or activities

❑ Getting more editors to run our press releases

❑ Planning and implementing a direct mail campaign or program

❑ Increasing direct mail response rates

❑ Generating low-cost but qualified leads using postcard decks

❑ How to make all our marketing communications more responsive and accountable

❑ Designing, writing, and producing a company newsletter

❑ Creating an effective company or capabilities brochure

❑ Developing strategies for responding to and following up on inquiries

❑ Creating effective inquiry fulfillment packages

❑ Producing and using a video or audio tape to promote our product or service

❑ Writing and publishing a book, booklet, or special report that can be used to promote our company or product

❑ Choosing an appropriate premium or advertising specialty as a customer giveaway

❑ Getting reviews and critiques of existing or in-progress copy for ads, mailings, brochures, and other promotions

❑ How to promote our product or service using free or paid seminars

❑ How to market our product or organization by having our people speak or present papers at conventions, trade shows, meetings, and other industry events

❑ Training our staff with an in-house seminar in:

_____
(indicate topic)

❑ Learning proven strategies for marketing our product or service in a recession or soft economy

❑ Other (describe): _____
_____
_____

– over –

(Continued)

Marketing Communications Audit

Step Two: Provide a Rough Indication of Your Budget

Amount of money you are prepared to commit to the solution of the problems checked off on page one of this form:

❑ under $500 ❑ under $1,000 ❑ under $2,500

❑ under $5,000 ❑ other: _____

Step Three: Fill in Your Name, Address, and Phone Number Below

Name _____ Title _____

Company _____ Phone _____

Address _____

City _____ State _____ Zip _____

Step Four: Mail or Fax Your Completed Form Today

Mail: Bob Bly, 174 Holland Avenue, New Milford, NJ 07646
FAX: (201) 599-2276
Phone: (201) 599-2277

If you wish, send me your current ads, brochures, mailing pieces, press releases, and any other material that will give me a good idea of the products or services you are responsible for promoting. I will review your audit and materials and provide a free 20-minute consultation by telephone with specific recommendations on how to solve your marketing problems, implement programs, and effectively address your key areas of concern. To schedule a specific date and time for your free, no-obligation phone consultation, indicate your preferred date and time below:

Preferred date and time _____

Alternate date and time _____

Mail your audit form today. There's no cost. And no obligation.

Bob Bly • Copywriter/Consultant • 22 Quackenbush Avenue, 3rd floor • Dumont, NJ 07628

SAMPLE PREPROGRAM
QUESTIONNAIRE FOR CLIENT TO COMPLETE

Preprogram Questionnaire

This questionnaire is designed to help us tailor our seminar to the specific needs, interests and background of the audience.

     Please answer each question as best you can and return this form to our office. Thanks!

1. Program you would like us to present for you:
❑ Effective technical writing
❑ Effective business writing.
❑ How to write copy that sells.
❑ How to use direct mail to generate more leads and sales.
❑ Selling your services.
❑ Successful selling.
❑ Keeping clients and customers satisfied.
❑ Fourteen ways to sell any product or service in a recession.
❑ Other:_____

2. Tell us a little more about the group.
Number of people who will be in the audience:_____
Average age:_____
Male/female ratio:_____
Annual personal income (if relevant):_____
Educational level:_____
Average number of years with company or organization:_ _____
Job titles/functions of people in the audience:
  1._____
  2._____
  3._____

3. Which of the following best describes the attitude of the majority of your audience toward our upcoming training session?
❑ Very eager and enthusiastic really looking forward to it.
❑ Somewhat eager and enthusiastic, if perhaps a tad skeptical about our ability to deliver something they can use.
❑ Neutral—neither enthusiastic nor skeptical—show-me attitude.
❑ Not terribly interested but not unhappy about going.
❑ Hostile, bored, or both—don't want to go and are being forced to by supervisor or manager.
❑ Smug—think they already know it all.
❑ Other:_____

(Continued)

(Continued)

4. How well educated is the audience in the topic of the seminar?

❑ They're all experts—the presentation should be advanced and on a high level.

❑ They're fairly knowledgeable but recognize there's always more to learn and room for improvement.

❑ They have some knowledge of the topic but haven't been exposed to it that much.

❑ They're novices and require a strong education in the fundamentals.

❑ Other: _____

5. What are the three most pressing challenges or problems faced by the members of your group?

1. _____
2. _____
3. _____

6. Which professional seminar leaders have you previously used to present programs on my topic?

1. _____
2. _____
3. _____

7. What are your specific objectives for our program? (What skills do you want your people to gain, what topics do you want to make sure we cover, etc.?)

1. _____
2. _____
3. _____
4. _____
5. _____

8. Are there any issues or topics that you want me to avoid during the program?

1. _____
2. _____
3. _____

9. Have you any other suggestions or advice to help me make this program your best ever?

1. _____
2. _____
3. _____

Instructions:

Please complete this form and mail it back to us at the address below.

Return to:

Bob Bly
Center for Technical Communication
22 East Quackenbush Avenue
Dumont, NJ 07628
Phone: 201-385-1220
Fax: 201-385-1138

SAMPLE SEMINAR EVALUATION FORM

Evaluation Form

1. Please rate the seminar:
❑ Excellent
❑ Very good
❑ Good
❑ Fair
❑ Poor

2. Please rate the instructors:
❑ Excellent
❑ Very good
❑ Good
❑ Fair
❑ Poor

3. What did you find most useful in the seminar? What did you like best?

4. What could be improved or added to make the program more useful to you?

Note: Your comments may be excerpted in our seminar announcement mailings.

Name _____

Title _____

Company _____

City _____

State _____ ZIP:_____

Web Sites

Copywriting Web Site
www.bly.com

How-to articles, books, resources
on copywriting.

Elance.com
www.elance.com

Web site linking consultants with
potential clients.

Management Consultant Network
www.mcninet.com

Professional resources for
management consultants.

Business Communication
www.espeakonline.com

How to communicate more
effectively in the Internet age.

Roger C. Parker
www.rcparker.com

How to create your own
successful Web site.

Working Relationships
www.customerrelations.com

Information on customer service,
customer care, and customer
relationships.

World Profit
www.worldprofit.com

Dr. Jeffrey Lant's Web site of
resources for entrepreneurs.

Consulting and Speaking Specialties and Industries

SPECIALTIES

Accounting
Acoustics
Actuary
Administration
Advertising—Consumer
Advertising—Industrial
Affirmative Action
Appraisal
Arbitration
Architecture
Association Management
Audit
Bankruptcy
Barter
Benefits
Call Centers
Cash Management
Collections
Communications

Compensation
Computer-Aided Design
Computer-Aided Engineering
Computer-Aided Manufacturing
Computer Hardware
Computer Software
Computer Training
Construction
Corporate Culture
Cost Analysis
Customer Service
Data Collection
Data Processing
Design
Direct Mail
Disaster Recovery
Distribution
Downsizing
Ecology

Economics
Empowerment
Energy
Engineering—Electrical
Engineering—Industrial
Engineering—Mechanical
Environment
Executive Search
Facilitation
Facilities
Factory Automation
Finance
Fire Prevention
Flood Control
Forecasting
Foreign Trade
Franchising
Fund-Raising
Heating/Air-Conditioning
Human Resources
Image
Import/Export
Industrial Development
Inspection
Insurance
Interim Personnel
Interior Design
Inventory
Investments
ISO 9000
Job Costing
Just-in-Time
Labor Relations
Leadership
Leasing
Lighting
Management
Management Information Systems
Manufacturing
Manufacturing Information
  Systems
Market Research

Marketing—Consumer
Marketing—Industrial
Marketing—International
Materials Handling
Materials Management
Media
Meetings
Merchandising
Mergers/Acquisitions
Metallurgy
Minority Affairs
Motivation
New Product Development
Office Automation
Organization
Outplacement
Packaging
Patents/Trademarks
Personnel
Planning
Politics
Polling
Pricing
Productivity
Project Management
Public Opinion
Public Policy
Pubic Relations
Publishing
Quality Assurance
Quality Control
Quantitative Analysis
Raw Materials
Recreation
Rehabilitation
Relocation
Renovation
Reorganization
Risk Management
Roofing
Safety
Sales Promotion

Sales Training
Sanitation
Scheduling
SEC Filings
Security
Simulation
Special Events
Statistics
Storage
Strategic Planning
Structural Design
Succession
System Design
Systems Analysis
Taxes
Team Building
Telecommunications
Telemarketing

Telephone Systems
Testing
Total Quality Management
Trade Shows
Training (other than computer or sales)
Transportation
Travel
Turnaround
Utilities
Value Engineering
Ventilation
Warehousing
Wholesaling
Workout
Writing
Other:

INDUSTRIES

Aerospace
Agriculture
Automotive
Aviation
Banking
Brokerage
Charities
Chemicals
Commodities
Communications
Computers
Construction
Consumer Electronics
Consumer Products
Data Processing
Distribution
Education
Electronics
Energy
Entertainment

Financial Services
Food and Beverage
Forestry
Government
Health and Beauty Aids
Health Care
Heating/Ventilation/
    Air-Conditioning
Import/Export
Insurance
Law
Leasing
Manufacturing
Media
Metals
Mining
Not-for-Profit
Packaging
Petroleum
Pharmaceuticals

Plastics
Raw Materials
Real Estate
Religion
Retailing
Services

Telecommunications
Textiles
Trade Associations
Transportation
Travel and Leisure
Other:

Credit Card Merchant Accounts

American Express
800-The-Card
Web site: www.americanexpress.
  com

Bancard, Inc.
1233 Sherman Drive
Longmont, CO 80501
800-666-7575

Cardserve West
4505 Las Vinges Road, #206
Calabasas, CA 91302
800-735-4171
Web site: www.cswcom.com
E-mail: cardo@cswcom.com

Data Capture Systems
231 Quincy Street
Rapid City, SD 57701
605-341-6461

Diners Club
800-2-Diners
Web site: www.citibank.com/
  dinersus

Discover
800-347-2683
Web site: www.discovercard.com

Electronic Bankcard Systems
2554 Lincoln Boulevard
Suite 1088
Marina Del Rey, CA 90291
213-827-5772

Electronic Credit Services
800-755-4327
Web site: www.ESCcards.com

Electronic Transfer Inc.
3107 East Mission
Spokane, WA 99202
800-757-3107

Elite Merchant Services
888-840-1079
Web site: www.elitecardservice.
  com
E-mail: info@elitecardservice.com

Frontline Processing Corporation
888-999-1523
Web site: www.frontlineprocessing.
  com

Gold Coast Bankcard Center
Fort Lauderdale, FL
305-492-0303

Harbridge Merchant Services
681 Andersen Drive, 4th Floor
Building 6
Pittsburgh, PA 15220
412-937-1272

MasterCard International
2000 Purchase Street
Purchase, NY 10577
914-249-2000
Web site: www.mastercard.com

1ClickCharge
Web site: www.1clickcharge.com

Specializes in low-dollar-amount
online credit card purchases.

Peachtree Software/World Wide
  Wallet
Web site: www.peachtree.com/os/

Teleflora Creditline
12233 West Olympic Boulevard
Los Angeles, CA 90064
800-32 S-4849
Web site: www.creditline.com

Total Merchant Services
100 Elk Run Drive, #225
Basair, CO 81621
888-84-TOTAL
E-mail: info@totalmerchant
  services.com

US Merchant Services
611 South Federal Highway
Stuart, FL 34994
561-220-7515
Web site: www.usmerchant
  services-inc.com

Visa International
P.O. Box 8999
San Francisco, CA 94128-8999
Web site: www.visa.com

Index